CW00796599

The ILO and the Social Challenges of the 21st Century:
The Geneva lectures

Studies in Employment and Social Policy

In the series Studies in Employment and Social Policy this book
The ILO and the Social Challenge of the 21st Century: The Geneva lectures
is the ninth title.

Studies in Employment and Social Policy

The ILO and the Social Challenges of the 21st Century:
The Geneva lectures

Edited by
Roger Blanpain & Chris Engels

P. Auer
D. Cunniah
J. Diller
T. Fashoyin
D. France
F. Hagemann
A.V. Jose
D. Kucera
S. Oates
A. Parisotto
J.-M. Servais
A. Trebilcock

2001
KLUWER LAW INTERNATIONAL
THE HAGUE/LONDON/BOSTON

Published by:
Kluwer Law International
P.O. Box 85889, 2508 CN The Hague, The Netherlands
sales@kli.wkap.nl
http://www.kluwerlaw.com

Sold and Distributed in North, Central and South America by:
Kluwer Law International
101 Philip Drive, Norwell, MA 02061, USA
kluwerlaw@wkap.com

Sold and Distributed in all other countries by:
Kluwer Law International
Distribution Centre, P.O. Box 322, 3300 AH Dordrecht, The Netherlands

Library of Congress Cataloging-in-Publication Data is available.

Printed on acid-free paper

ISBN 90-411-1572-2
© 2001 Kluwer Law International

Kluwer Law International incorporates the publishing programs
of Graham & Trotman Ltd, Kluwer Law and Taxation Publishers
and Martinus Nijhoff Publishers

Printed and bound in Great Britain by MPG Books Ltd., Bodmin, Cornwall.

CONTENTS

Contents

INTRODUCTORY REMARKS

This book has its roots in the former World Conference of the International Society of Labour Law and Social Security, which was held in 1963 in Lyon, France, under the flamboyant chairmanship of Professor André Brun. There I made my first intervention at an international conference on the theme of Trade Union Freedom for which Professor Clyde Summers, Yale University, USA, was the general reporter. I expanded on the Belgian system, on the positive and negative freedom of association and especially on the benefit reserved for trade union members only, which is a unique feature of the Belgian industrial relations system. My remarks referred to the ILO standards concerning freedom of association and collective bargaining. This prompted a reaction by one of the leading officers of the ILO, at that time, Mr. Jean de Givry. He explained that the ILO standards only considered positive freedom of association and were silent on the negative freedom of association. These interventions lead to contacts between Mr. de Givry and myself, whereby I invited him to give a lecture to my labour law students at the Faculty of Law of the Catholic University of Leuven in Belgium. At the end of his visit, Mr. De Givry extended an invitation to me to visit the ILO. All of these events had greatly stimulated my interest to learn more about the ILO.

It was then 1964 and the ILO was still situated in its original building at Lake Geneva, where the World Trade Organisation is currently housed. I spent several days at the ILO, meeting various civil servants. Coming from a small country like Belgium, I was impressed by the worldwide vision and scope of action of the ILO.

When I left Geneva after this first visit I decided that I had to share this unique and everlasting experience with my students. And so, with the kind co-operation of the staff of the ILO, a program of lectures and discussions was set up, starting for the first time in 1965. It would be the start of a long tradition.

The usual programme includes about 35 students who attend lectures and have the opportunity for discussion over a four-day period. A visit to the UN headquarters is included. Lecturers were staff of the ILO and/of the International Institute for Social Studies, as well as the representatives of the International Employers Organisation and the International Trade Unions, such as the ICFTU, the IMF and FIET. A visit to the extra-ordinary ILO library is self-evidently a must.

From the very beginning, the Belgian Embassy played a very important role, not only by hosting a reception for the students, but also by organising a meeting with the staff of the Embassy, who would explain their duties in Geneva, not only in the ILO, but also in other international bodies or conferences like the UN, the WHO, disarmament, WIPO, the links between the EU and the ILO and so on.

In a week's time, a kind of miracle takes place. Students get an international outlook, an open door to the world, a new vision putting issues in perspective, making their own problems look small in comparison to those on other continents. It changes their mindset almost completely. The fact that most of our meetings could take place in the ILO headquarters themselves added to this overwhelming international happening.

There is no doubt that many international careers were inspired by this grand tour, which the ILO hosted over 35 years to more than 1000 students that I am privileged to accompany. Many assistants accompanied me on our yearly visit and became permanently involved in the ILO, like Johanna Walgrave and Danny Duyssens. Others are now ambassadors, consuls-general, etc. We are now welcoming a second generation of students, whose mothers and fathers before them made the trip as students.

We have developed lasting relationships with many of the ILO officials and other speakers. Let me just name a few of them (at the risk of forgetting many): Nicolas Valticos, Johannes Schregle, Alan Gladstone, Jean Jacques Oeschlin, Hans Gunther, Hector G. Bartolomei de la Cruz, Father Joblin, Alfred Pankert, Jean-Michel Servais, M. Ozaki, Michel Hansenne, Kari Tapiola, Tayo Fashoyin and others. These relationships led to new research projects, organised by the ILO, or within the framework of the International Encyclopaedia for Labour Law and Industrial Relations and of the International Industrial Relations Association, when I had the honour of being President of the IIRA (1986–1989) and Alan Gladstone was its very efficient Secretary-General. Today this working relationship continues through the International Association of Labour Law and Social Security of which Jean-Michel Servais is the Secretary-General.

The present Belgian Ambassador, Mr. J.M. Noirfalise, and his staff deserve a special mention for their unique and generous contribution.

Over the years the composition of our group of students has changed. Since the Erasmus programme, our law faculties have become Europeanised if not internationalised. As a consequence, our group has become one in which more than 10 countries are represented, adding to the international atmosphere of the visit.

With the passing of time I have become a professor emeritus in Leuven and my successor, Professor Chris Engels, has taken over and continues the good tradition of bringing his students to Geneva. I'm still part of the group and enjoy the company of some of my students in Tilburg, the Netherlands, where I teach at present. I hope the tradition will continue.

We are extremely grateful to the ILO, the International Institute for Labour Studies and to the many friends in Geneva for their contribution to the enlightenment of our students, making them world citizens.

After our most recent visit in March 2000, we reflected on how we could share this experience with an even larger audience. Thus, the decision was made, together with the speakers, that we would publish their texts under the title "The Geneva lectures". A reason to be even more grateful.

This book thus contains the lectures given by prominent civil servants and representatives of the International Employers' Association (IOE) and the International

Confederation of Free Trade Unions to law students from various European countries at the occasion of their visit to the International Labour Organisation. The purpose of these lectures is to expand on the major problems the ILO, as the social conscience of the world, will be confronted with in the next century. These lectures open a multitude of global trends, which will determine the future outlook of our societies.

The Geneva lectures deal with the following important topics:

- the world of work
- the informal economy
- globalisation and the confrontation it involves
- the future of the trade union movement
- the role of the employer's associations
- the ILO Declaration on fundamental principles and rights at work (1998)
- child labour
- international labour standards
- the codes of conduct of multinational enterprises

We are extremely grateful to P. Auer, D. Cunniah, J. Diller, T. Fashoyin, D. France, F. Hagemann, A.V. Jose, D. Kucera, S. Oates, A. Parisotto, J.-M. Servais and A. Trebilcock, for their stimulating lectures and for having made the effort and taken the time to make this book possible. They give the reader insight to the world of tomorrow and how one of the leading international bodies reflects on how to deal with it.

This book is dedicated to all those, who over the years have introduced our students to the international world of work and its quest for social justice.

Roger Blanpain

NOTES ON CONTRIBUTORS

PETER AUER
Head, Labour Market Team, Employment Strategy Department, ILO, *auer@ilo.org*

ROGER BLANPAIN
Professor European and Comparative Labour Law, Universities of Leuven (Belgium) and Tilburg (The Netherlands), President of the International Society for Labour Law and Social Security, *roger.blanpain@cer-leuven.be*

DAN CUNNIAH
Director, Geneva Office of the International Confederation of Free Trade Unions and Secretary of the Workers' Group of the ILO Governing Body, *dan.cunniah@geneva.icftu.org*

JANELLE M. DILLER
Head, Private Voluntary Initiatives Program, ILO, *diller@ilo.org*

CHRIS ENGELS
Professor European and Comparative Labour Law, Social Procedural Law and Industrial Relations, University of Leuven (Belgium), Lawyer admitted at the Brussels Bar, Belgium, Partner Claeys & Engels, *chris.engels@claeysengels.be*

TAYO FASHOYIN
Officer in Charge, InFocus Programme on Strengthening Social Dialogue, ILO, *fashoyin@ilo.org*

DEBORAH FRANCE
Deputy Secretary-General, International Organisation of Employers, *france@ioe-emp.org*

FRANK HAGEMANN
Policy Analyst, International Programme on the Elimination of Child Labour (IPEC), ILO, *hagemann@ilo.org*

VARKEY JOSE
Head, Labour and Society Programme, International Institute for Labour Studies, ILO, *jose@ilo.org*

Notes on Contributors

DAVID KUCERA
Senior Research Officer, International Institute for Labour Studies, ILO,
kucera@ilo.org

STEVEN OATES
Programming Coordinator in the International Labour Standards and Fundamental
Principles and Rights Sector, ILO, *oates@ilo.org*

AURELIO PARISOTTO
Head, Education and Outreach Programme, International Institute for Labour
Studies, ILO, *parisotto@ilo.org*

JEAN MICHEL SERVAIS
Research Coordinator at the International Institute for Labour Studies (ILO),
Secretary-General of the International Society for Labour Law and Social Security,
servais@ilo.org

ANNE TREBILCOCK
Director, Reports and Research, InFocus Programme on Promoting the
Declaration, ILO, *trebilcock@ilo.org*

Aurelio Parisotto

1. ECONOMIC GLOBALISATION AND THE DEMAND FOR DECENT WORK

1. INTRODUCTION

This visit of students has been held regularly for many years. I am particularly happy that this year, for the first time, the visit takes place under the auspices of the International Institute for Labour Studies. For us at the Institute, this is a significant way to inaugurate the emphasis we want to place on renewing and strengthening partnership between the ILO and the academic and student communities of the world.

As in the past, the programme of lectures has been set up so as to provide an overview of ILO activities. The three lectures that will be delivered on the first day of the programme will draw upon the research work done at the International Institute for Labour Studies. Their aim, in line with the mission of the Institute within the ILO, will be to review and explore scenarios for social policy and to identify emerging challenges for the ILO, its constituents and all those who have an interest in social and labour issues. We thought that this was the necessary groundwork and, hopefully, a stimulating prelude to the rest of the programme. Long-standing ILO concerns with internationally recognised human and labour rights will be dealt with on the second day, by means of looking at traditional and new ILO instruments, respectively the international labour standards and the Declaration on Fundamental Principles and Rights at Work and its Follow-up. Policy matters relating to employment creation and industrial relations will be touched upon on the third day, while on the last day we will discuss examples of what the ILO does concretely to promote its principles, in particular through its technical cooperation programmes targeted to fight child labour and through its efforts to support voluntary private social initiatives.

Our hope is that, by the end of this cycle of lectures, you will have a comprehensive view of the context for ILO action and the rationale behind its strategy and its new programme orientations.

* * *

This year's visit of student occurs at a special juncture in the history of the ILO.

R. Blanpain and C. Engels (eds), The ILO and the Social Challenge of the 21st Century, 1–10.
© 2001 *Kluwer Law International. Printed in Great Britain.*

The Office is currently engaged in a major reorientation of its programmes and structures to reflect the new strategic framework proposed by its new Director-General, the first from outside the industrialised world. The new ILO agenda was spelt out for the first time in the Director-General's report on Decent Work, endorsed by the International Labour Conference in June 1999. In it, the Director-General described the primary role of the ILO as the promotion of *"opportunities for women and men to obtain decent and productive work, in conditions of freedom, equity, security and human dignity"*.[1] In order to enable the Office to respond to the global demand for decent work in a balanced and integrated way, and within the framework of the fundamental values that have guided the work of the ILO since its creation, he also proposed to reorganise ILO activities around four strategic objectives – namely, the promotion of fundamental rights and principles at work; employment; social protection; and social dialogue.

Thus, this cycle of lectures captures the reality of the ILO at a time of transition, a period in which on-going programmes are being redefined, new programmes are launched, and organisational structures are realigned to attend to a new set of operational priorities.

The main purpose of my talk is to sketch out a few simple facts about current trends that are shaping the world of work: the growth of multinational enterprises; technological change and the information revolution; workers' migration and demographic pressures; and the pressure of public opinion to move away from national deregulation and international "unregulation". These trends are elements of a major transformation, commonly referred to as globalisation, that is shaping our world in complex and uneven ways. If we look at these trends, we could argue that globalisation – which has been advancing rapidly in recent years – is likely to gain even further momentum in the years ahead. At the same time, public support for its expansion is declining.

The first flush of globalisation was driven largely by absolute faith in market forces. Today, following a series of financial, social and political crises in several regions of the world, the policy attitude is changing. There is growing concern that the benefits of globalisation may be more volatile than expected and that they have accrued only to a very limited extent to those who need them most. Growing economic insecurity and the failure to deliver significant developmental outcomes to a very large portion of the world's population – first and foremost enough work opportunities to meet people's aspirations to a decent life – is prompting many to question the policies, the institutional structures and the ideological stance that have governed the process of globalisation so far. Many precariously-placed individuals and communities, in particular, see globalisation as "a terrorising prospect" (Sen, 1999, p.1).

Such failure is raising the attention of public opinion and policy-makers towards the values and the approaches for which the ILO has consistently stood since its establishment in 1919. After many years during which the focus was exclusively on growth and stabilisation, the watershed in international thinking started at the World Summit for Social Development, held in Copenhagen in March 1995, when 117 heads of state stressed the importance of equity, participation, empowerment and solidarity. They also gave a special role to the ILO in the field of employment and social development. In my concluding remarks, I will suggest that the new ILO agenda, built around the notion of "decent work", stemmed from the need to take the ILO message forward in the context of the economic and social transformations brought about by the emerging global economy. The social policy debate at the national and international levels is currently dominated by the need to grasp the economic opportunities offered by globalisation while, at the same time, coping with the social challenges it poses. "Decent work" is a tool to achieve such a task in the most beneficial manner for people everywhere.

2. Growing Global Connections and the Labour Market

These are times of rapid, pervasive and relentless change in economy and society. As never before, change is affecting all countries and all groups of workers. Yet, there is one central element: more ties, and more complex ones, are linking people living in different parts of the world. We enjoy goods and services coming from far away countries. We communicate and send e-mails across the planet. We are informed about events taking place in remote corners and take a stance that may affect them. Our lives and our jobs are influenced by decisions taken at the other end of the globe. Globalisation could be described as a set of processes leading to an advanced state of economic, social and political interdependence between different countries and regions of the world. The exponential growth of these global connections is a distinctive feature of its current phase.[2]

Interdependence brings about volatility. Very high levels of interdependence and volatility, for instance, are found on the financial markets. Most countries are incorporated into one global financial market and are exposed to its vagaries; perturbations taking place in one place reverberate round the entire system, as shown by the international effects of the collapse of the Thai Bath in 1997. Interdependence and volatility also constrain national economic and social policies. Financial markets expectations influence key variables such as interests rates and fiscal budgets. This induces national policy-makers to adopt risk-adverse policy approaches, such as tight social expenditure and conservative macroeconomic strategies that do not maximise the possibilities for growth and employment generation.

As concerns product markets, the number of countries that participate in international trade is higher than ever. Similarly, the world has never been more open to foreign direct investments. This has created unprecedented opportunities for growth and employment generation. Some economies in the developing world, in particular in Asia, have been able to gain skilfully from greater access to international markets to achieve fast rates of economic growth and significantly higher income levels. Yet the crises in Asia, Russia and Brazil have shown how the benefits of globalisation could be volatile and how vast numbers of people could be rapidly pushed back into

3

poverty where economic expansion is not supported by the development of adequate social protection systems.

Everywhere, economic growth has been accompanied by an increasing feeling of vulnerability for people, a sentiment exacerbated by the weakening of social institutions, such as the welfare state and trade unions. Where jobs have been created, they have often been of a poor quality. Employment in informal economic activities has grown both in the North and the South, reaching record levels of as much as 80 per cent of the new jobs generated in Africa and Latin America in recent years. Not everybody has benefited from the new economic trend. Countries in Central and Eastern Europe continue to suffer; Latin American countries have experienced economic and social drawbacks; and large parts of the world's population have been excluded, as shown most remarkably by the social and political collapse of Africa.

The above asymmetries in the distribution of benefits have aggravated deep-seated inequalities and development problems that pre-existed globalisation. In spite of productivity increases and technological marvels, one third of the world's population still lives in absolute poverty, i.e. they are excluded from access to minimum economic security, education, safety and health. In short, there is a global deficit in the quantity and quality of the opportunities that people in all countries have to work and conduct a decent life. Unless a response is given to this demand, public deception with the current process of globalisation will grow and their resistance to greater openness its likely to mount.

3. THE DRIVING FORCES

Several factors are driving the current process of economic integration. Some of them account for its further expansion, creating enormous opportunities while, at the same time, intensifying labour market tensions and posing new policy questions.

3.1. Multinational Enterprises and Global Production Networks

Over 60,000 multinational enterprises (MNEs), up from about 7,000 in the 1970s, account for about one quarter of world production and two thirds of international trade. In spite of its size, the multinational enterprises system accounts, on the whole, for a small and stagnating number of jobs: the total employment in the MNEs at home and abroad is estimated to be around 3 per cent of the world work force (UNCTAD, 1999, chapter I). To evaluate its importance to global economic prosperity, we should consider that MNEs are active in the most dynamic and knowledge-intensive nodes of the value chain in most industries. They have access to critical resources such as capital, production capabilities and information, and are the masters of organisational change and human resource development.

Equally important, MNEs link very large numbers of smaller independent enterprises into globally coordinated production and distribution networks, acting as a driving force much like the nervous system in a human body. Large well-established

MNEs – the tip of the iceberg of these networks – concentrate on activities such as research, product development, marketing, advertising, financing, and legal protection of copyright, while leaving manufacturing production to expanding layers of international suppliers and subcontractors dispersed all over the world.[3] These networks have raised economic interdependence to new levels, by knitting together firms regardless of their location, acting as main channels for the international transfer of technology, and allowing even small producers in remote and poor corners of the world to gain some access to the international market. Their operations open up potential opportunities for jobs, transfer of technology, and some local learning and emulation processes, which are very important, especially for poor countries, and explain the eagerness of governments to attract greater foreign investments and international outsourcing.

The companies at the top of these networks have vast resources and an enormous geographical reach. Influential decisions are taken in their boardrooms. They are less footloose than it is usually thought, but their exit power – the threat to withdraw investment from a country – is considerable. To bargain with them on a equal footing is out of the reach of many single nation states.

3.2. *Technological Change and the Information Revolution*

Rapid decline in the costs of transportation and telecommunications has made it more feasible and convenient than ever to move capital, goods and knowledge across national boundaries, allowing enterprises to take advantage of foreign markets and enhancing their capabilities to closely coordinate geographically dispersed activities. The most recent advances in information and communications technologies (ICTs) may push economic integration much further ahead.

There are about 300 million Internet users worldwide today. The projected growth is up to one billion by 2005.[4] The information revolution, led by the sharp decline in the price of information processing, the convergence in communication and computing technologies, and the rapid growth of the Internet, is opening up outstanding potential opportunities to conduct business across national boundaries. We are nearing a world in which telephone calls could be made at zero cost while, at the same time, the amount of information that can be transmitted in digital forms is increasing exponentially. Many products and services could soon be efficiently delivered on-line. Others could be despatched through conventional distribution systems, but the information-intensive dimensions of each transaction could be conducted electronically, e.g. market search, product information and payment.

Several industries are already experiencing deep restructuring with major implications for their workers; e.g finance, banking, media and entertainment, business services, tourism, wholesale and retail distribution. This wave is affecting economies in the developed and the developing world: for instance, services such as data entry, accounting, processing of insurance and medical forms, on-line software assistance are being decentralised electronically to poor income countries in India, the

5

Philippines, Barbados, Costa Rica, and Senegal. In all industries, new efficient business practices are emerging. All kinds of enterprises are rethinking their approach to strategy and organisation, using the new communications systems to reconstruct their supply chains and redesign their relationships with customers and employees. Small independent businesses are using the new network communications opportunities to access lucrative niches of the global market, while large MNEs are using intranets, extranets and the Internet to link more closely their design, procurement, manufacturing, logistics and marketing worldwide. From their central purchase offices, the new practices could spread out to smaller firms in all corners of their vast networks of production and distribution.

There is great excitement as well as great concern among the business community and policy-makers in developed and developing countries for the implications of the information society. Three policy areas in particular are attracting the attention of policy-makers. The first relates to the need to develop national and international regulatory and technological frameworks to let digital transactions take place efficiently, without risk, and with maximum benefit to people. Issues range from technical standards to taxation, security, censorship, copyright, privacy and access. The second policy concern is to ensure that firms and workers are equipped to take advantage of the new opportunities to compete and grow which are offered by ICTs. One main facet is the unprecedented emphasis given to education and training. In the economy as it is now taking shape, human resources are the key asset for industrial success. It is no surprise that education and the development of skills are becoming the cornerstone of employment policies in many parts of the world.

The third, and most challenging, concern is to narrow the growing "digital divide" between, on the one hand, those who have the resources, the education, the social approval and the institutions to sign up for the information revolution and, on the other hand, those who are excluded. One half of the world's population have never made a telephone call. Only 12 per cent of Internet users are within developing and transition economies. (UNDP, 1999). Getting connected to the new information networks provides incredible resources to firms and individuals; the absence of links is just as definitively an incredible disadvantage. Differences in the access to the new technologies and the capability to use them effectively are self-sustaining and generate growing disparities. Countries that have reached a certain threshold may fare well, but for the vast majority of the developing world to ensure that people get "connected" is much beyond the resources and capabilities at their disposal.

3.3. Migration and Demography

In the age of globalisation there remain great barriers to the circulation of people across national borders. Economic migration is increasingly common and has a less permanent nature for special groups, e.g. highly skilled and specialised workers. But for most workers it is a difficult and strongly regulated option. Migration has a direct and clearly visible impact on the fabric of societies. While it is recognised that there are positive effects for both receiving and sending countries over the long term, host communities are resistant to new arrivals. Large uncontrolled inflows of people produce undesirable social frictions with significant political consequences.

Nonetheless the total number of migrants around the world now surpasses 120 million – up from 75 million in 1965 – and continues to grow (Stalker, 2000). Government interference has little impact on the total number of migrants worldwide, but it affects migration patterns and it spurs illegal trafficking. There are fundamental labour market forces that are leading to growing international migration and, by this token, to growing interdependence. They have to do with divergent demographic trends across regions. In the less developed countries, high fertility rates account for a doubling of the population every 42 years, generating gigantic numbers of young people looking for a work opportunity (PRB, 2000). In the more developed countries the rate of growth of the population is close to zero, so that severe shortages in the supply of workers are estimated to occur pretty soon. This divergence is generating a tension like that preceding the thunderstorm – either people will migrate to the North in search of working opportunities, or jobs will have to move in some form to the South.

3.4. Towards a More Balanced Policy Drive?

Significant reductions in tariffs and other regulatory barriers in almost every country over the past two decades have paved the way to the spreading of global market forces. As a matter of fact, liberalisation and deregulation have become coterminous with globalisation in the perception of the public opinion. But public support to these policies is weakening and there are visible signs of dissatisfaction with the social and labour implications of the current process of globalisation. People's concern emerges across disparate segments of society. It is not limited to the labour market; it also touches on issues relating to environmental protection and national cultural identity. The movement against globalisation has a truly multinational dimension, fostered by easiness of communications and growing awareness of the interconnections. In its quest for participation in international politics, it targets specifically those institutions that are perceived as having main tasks of global governance. Its most significant upshot has been to prevent further multilateral liberalisation of trade and investment, as exemplified by the failure of the World Trade Organisation (WTO) ministerial conference in Seattle in late 1999.

One effect of the protest in Seattle has been that the need to pay more attention to the social dimension of the economic change seems more firmly established in the language of international policy. There is a growing common feeling that newly conceived national and international policies should to be adopted to set the globalisation process on a new, more sustainable and equitable course. But the winning of the language has not translated into policy action yet. It goes much beyond our purposes to try to analyse the reasons. One simple aspect is that policy-making has become more difficult and complex. Traditional tools of economic and social policy are less effective in the context of global competition. Not only is the technical side of economic and social policies more complex, demands are greater. National governments are squeezed between global forces and growing local demands, and their room for manoeuvring has changed. They must operate more sophisticated strategies than before, and be involved in more complex negotiations. At the local level, for instance, they have to accommodate demands for greater autonomy or, paradoxically, stimulate those demands by acting as catalysts for local self-governing institutions – effective local institutions capable to mobilise local knowledge are proving to be major instruments in implementing effective schemes for poverty alleviation and small business development.

At the international level, governments have increasingly to deploy their power and authority as bargaining chips in multilateral and transnational negotiations, as they must collaborate and coordinate with other governments and international agencies, or confront transnational actors from business and civil society. Today, more than 4,000 international summits convene each year, compared to two or three congresses 150 years ago (Helm, ib. p. 487). This explosion of supranational fora is signalling the emergence of a multi-layered system of global governance, formal and informal. Its significance is likely to increase as globalisation and interdependence advance further. It is probably wrong to claim the end of the nation states. Political power, taxation and military force remain strongly linked to circumscribed territories, where mechanisms of democratic control exist, but "the practical nature of this entitlement – the actual capacity of states to rule – is changing its shape" (Helm et al., p. 495). While there is a need for a more activist state, there is uncertainty about what exactly its role and functions should be, which results in a lot of policy experiments.

4. Concluding Remarks

There are strong forces pressing for deeper international economic integration. They stem from the desire of enterprises and governments – both in rich and poor nations – to exploit competitive advantage and access new markets. They are likely to receive additional impetus as a result of unprecedented advance in information and communication technologies. They are going to be compounded by uncontrollable movements of workers across national boundaries. We should, therefore, look ahead at times of great turbulence as well as opportunity. The implications for the labour markets will be far-reaching and multi-faceted. Jobs will be created in some sectors and countries while declining sharply in others; the content and geography of work will change for many people; unprecedented increases in productivity will arise together with old and new inequalities. In an increasingly interconnected world, the social tensions that this might create will not stop at a single country's national borders.

The opposition to globalisation has had the merit to pose the question of the policies that should govern this process. It has also called into question the efficacy and the accountability of the international institutions that are mandated to support and monitor those policies. The on-going global transformation of our world will have to be better managed if we want to have greater benefits from it and secure its social sustainability. Much could be done, at both the national and international levels, to grasp the benefits of globalisation while minimising the social distress it creates. National policies in the domain of small business development, education and training, protection and empowerment of the poor are some examples of initiatives that could be implemented regardless of globalisation. They would be even more effective, in particular in the poorest countries, if they could enjoy international support in an enabling international environment. Other questions – such as the volatility of speculative capital flows; the race for investments; the emergence of a "digital divide" between rich and poor countries; the pressure of demography and the problems of international migration – are everybody's responsibility. They clearly require international coordination and international action. But, inertia, conflicts and unprecedented complexity combine to make the shift to a new policy drive hesitant and slow.

The response of the International Labour Office is summarised in the notion of "decent work". Decent work builds on the fundamental values that have inspired and guided the work of the ILO since its creation: the promotion of human and labour rights and the enhancement of the welfare of workers. Its new distinctive feature is the effort to integrate this long-standing value-based agenda into a sustainable development agenda based on "jobs, enterprise creation and human resources enhancement" (ILO, 2000, p. 1).

In the decent work agenda, to expand jobs and working opportunities is a central objective to fight poverty and exclusion. At the same time, the conditions of work and life are equally important: economic and social progress could hardly be sustained if those who work are not given dignity, a decent standard of living, respect for their rights at work, and the means to express their voice. To generate opportunities for decent work is not simply a matter of adopting expansionary economic policies. It rather requires integrated policies to foster job creation while promoting respect for the fundamental rights of workers, providing basic protection for them and their families, and furthering social dialogue. This calls for policy innovation and new research to identify virtuous circles and win-win initiatives that could simultaneously foster economic and social efficiency.

The coverage of the decent work goal is momentously large. It includes *all* women and men; not just wage workers in the formal labour market, but also unregulated wage workers, the self-employed, and the homeworkers. This implies that attention should be paid to all groups of the working population, and that trade-offs between the interests of one group or the other – when they exist – should be addressed by taking an inclusive approach.[5] Such a comprehensive objective could not be achieved without mobilising, around the ILO's tripartite core constituency, the energy of a plurality of actors from business and society by means of new partnerships and new solidarities at the national and international levels.

To conclude, to set "decent work" as the ILO's primary objective could be seen as

9

an attempt to focus the emerging international policy agenda on the issue of work; and to emphasise that the most urgent task is to create more and better job opportunities and to enhance human capabilities and social capital. The "decent work" agenda summarises the renewed attention given by policy-makers and public opinion to the social dimension of markets. It calls for an integration of economic and social policies; it advocates new partnerships between states, markets and civil society; and it is intended to provide inspiration for more effective international collective action. It is a tool to help fulfil, in cooperation and coordination with national constituents and other international agencies, the responsibility for employment and social issues given to the ILO by the international community. It is the start of a difficult and necessary endeavour.

BIBLIOGRAPHY

D. Held and A. McGrew, with D. Goldblatt and J. Perraton, "Globalization", *Global Governance*, Vol. 5, No. 4, Oct–Dec 1999.
ILO. *"Decent Work for All"*, address of the Director-General to the staff of the World Bank, 2 March 2000, see: www.ilo.org/public/english/bureau/dgo/speeches/somavia/2000/worldbk.htm.
ILO, *Decent Work*, Report of the Director-General to the International Labour Conference, 87th Session, Geneva, 1999. see also www.ilo.org/public/english/standards/relm/ilc/ilc87/rep-i.htm.
Population Reference Bureau, *2000 World Population Data Sheet*, Washington DC, 2000.
A. Sen, *Address to the International Labour Conference, 87th session*, 15 June 1999, see http://www.ilo.org/public/english/standards/relm/ilc/ilc87/a-sen.htm.
P. Stalker, *Workers without frontiers – The impact of globalization on international migration*, ILO, Geneva 2000.
UNCTAD, *World Investment Report 1999: Investment and the Challenge of Development*, Geneva, 1999.
UNDP, *Human Development Report 1999*, New York, Oxford University Press, 1999.

NOTES

1   ILO, 1999, p. 3.
2   See Held et al., p. 483
3   A company like Nike, for example, employs directly about 10,000 workers. But its total system of satellite and independent suppliers accounts for some 500,000 jobs.
4   *ACM TechNews* Volume 2, Issue 34, 24 March 2000.
5   The case for such a broad focus is discussed in Sen, 1999, who also highlights three other key conceptual features of the "decent work" approach: the idea of rights; the underlying vision of society; and its truly global nature.

Jean-Michel Servais

2. THE FUTURE OF WORK AND RELATED SECURITY: A DISCUSSION OF THE NEED TO PLACE MATTERS IN PERSPECTIVE

1. INTRODUCTION: THE NEW FEATURES OF PRODUCTION AND ORGANISATION OF WORK

Increased trade flows and capital mobility are transforming the organisation of work and modifying labour–management relationships. While the advent of globalisation is not necessarily leading to a large-scale industrial migration of firms fleeing high labour costs and taxes, it is generating increasing options for firms to maintain or relocate manufacturing investment. The mere existence of that option, combined with new technologies and methods of organisation, is having a broad impact on enterprise culture: for countries, enterprises and individuals alike, economic openness means adjusting to change.

One can identify three principal changes in the organisation of work which result from capital mobility – a reduced margin of manoeuvre for governments; greater autonomy for enterprises; and increased competition with regard to wages. The International Labour Organisation (ILO) has emphasised that these factors will need to be dealt with by evolving systems of industrial relations if the growth of economic inequality is to be reversed and if globalisation is to prove politically and economically sustainable.[1]

If globalisation and technological innovations have potential positive consequences for growth and employment, they also have potentially destabilising effects upon the distribution of wealth and the collective bargaining process. Capital mobility destabilises the sheltered structure of wages that national industrial relations systems produced when market competition was largely a national matter. In many respects, the result is beneficial: increased competition drives productivity, encourages firms to be more cost-sensitive, generates high-paying investments in technology and innovation and holds down inflation. With greater locational choice, the cost of labour is on the negotiating table; wages, once taken out of competition, are now back in the competitive sphere. The problem affects low-skilled labour in particular which becomes readily available to enterprises once they have a certain degree of locational freedom.

R. Blanpain and C. Engels (eds), The ILO and the Social Challenge of the 21st Century, 11–29.
© 2001 *Kluwer Law International. Printed in Great Britain.*

Trade competition and capital mobility can thus have the effect of dividing workers at the national level. Capital mobility rewards very qualified workers, given that mobile capital seeks them out and bids up their wages, but the contrary is true for the less skilled who used to be protected from wage competition. Efforts by trade unions to boost the wages and conditions of less-skilled workers can also meet with greater resistance. By making firms more sensitive to labour costs, capital mobility can also make them more sensitive to union organising campaigns.

The attempt to attract investment capital can also produce important behavioural changes in the exercise of freedom of association or in the industrial relations climate. Examples may include the United Kingdom during the inflow, in the 1980s, of Japanese investments; a form of pre-investment bargaining occurred which had the effect of transforming traditional industrial relations practices, notably single union recognition arrangements and no-strike clauses in collective bargaining agreements. Decisions on car industry investment in Latin America were often made contingent on prior trade union assent to conditions demanded by firms.

In reducing the independence of national macroeconomic policy, globalisation enhances a firm's role as the primary engine of wealth and job creation. At the same time, it exposes the firm to heightened competition. It erodes the shelter in which firms used to operate and makes flexibility essential for responding to rapid product-market changes. Enterprises have responded by transforming how they organise work and production. In the process, industrial relations at the enterprise level have taken on greater importance.

The effort to promote flexibility and "lean" production has led to reduction in management layers. In many cases, these managers' responsibilities have been transferred directly to the shop-floor where technological innovations and information systems have reduced overall manufacturing employment and new methods of organisation – such as cross-functional teams and multiskilling – have radically changed the nature of employment. The process of downsizing and reorganising work has transformed the traditional system of highly segmented jobs and rigid job descriptions that prevailed as recently as the early 1980s in a number of industrialised countries.

While these new methods offer certain advantages to workers in the form of greater autonomy, responsibility and decision-making power, the benefits have frequently been offset by higher unemployment, reduced employment security, limited career prospects and a growing percentage of peripheral workers on casual, temporary or part-time contracts.

Existing industrial relations structures have, in many cases, been circumvented by new phenomena known generically as human resources management (HRM) policies. They may cover the organisation of teamwork, training, payment systems, employee participation and personnel policy but do not yet appear to have resolved the tensions inherent in labour–management relationships. They do not address the treatment of trade unions and collective agreements.

These policies are sometimes introduced in collaboration with trade unions, particularly in Japan and Germany; in other cases, however, the collective representation bodies are not consulted. In the final analysis, the architecture of future industrial relations will be largely determined by how employers and workers resolve the tension between cooperation-based policies, including HRM, and traditional industrial relations based on the collective representation of workers. The two need to be complementary for a number of reasons.

First, cooperation-based policies that rely on the dedication and commitment of employees and hence on the need to ensure a certain level of employment stability only relate to part of the workforce. Because there is also evidence of increasing recourse to precarious forms of employment, it will prove difficult in the absence of collective representation for workers with a precarious status to derive similar benefits to those enjoyed by full-time workers. Some problems will remain immune to direct cooperation-based solutions and recourse to other forums, including trade unions, will remain necessary.

Second, the innovations have so far been diffused in a restrictive and uneven manner. The results obtained and the changes implemented by HRM style solutions will vary greatly from country to country. Finally, industrial organisations, and in particular workers' organisations, frequently have to confront issues that extend beyond the boundaries of enterprises and, for these, collective forums for negotiation will prove necessary, be it at the local, sectoral or national levels. They should assist in particular in giving answers to the present social malaise.

2. The New Social Question

2.1. *Social Instability and New Insecurities*

Social systems are naturally founded on basic rules designed to establish the living environment of their members. These may be moral or religious principles. When such principles are no longer sufficient, the State itself seeks to impose its own standards and penalties for this purpose. However, if the social and economic context changes, the principles in question must be adapted. We are probably living through an age of change with the technological revolution and the acceleration of the process of economic globalisation. Whatever the case may be, social links are being broken in many different places.

In schools, the lack of communication and mutual understanding between pupils and teachers is being denounced. In cities both large and small, insecurity, violence and delinquency are assuming a political dimension owing to their sheer scale; to an extent, social conflicts have left factories and have been transplanted to poor neighbourhoods and the public transport serving those neighbourhoods. Families are also undergoing upheavals: latent opposition or open confrontation between parents and children; parents often "giving in"; the increase in problems between partners in cases where women affirm their legitimate right to their own careers; the interests of men and women diverge and require a greater effort towards reconciliation of the personal aspirations of both spouses.

Certain mass events create a stir, for example the reactions to the death of Diana, Princess of Wales or, a few years ago in Brussels, the so-called "white" protest march against all established authority in Belgium, reflect sentiments which are difficult to assess in rational terms. With the aid of the media, they probably express anguish and frustration projected onto individuals whose charisma does not correspond to any kind of totally convincing explanation.

However, the ever-more precarious nature of work, under-employment and the absence of employment probably constitute the main reasons for the destabilisation of social relations. In Japan, an unemployment rate of above four per cent gives rise to real fears that the current depression will seriously affect the type of society built by this country since the Second World War. This rate is in no way comparable to those reached in Europe, however, or worse still in developing countries, where the situation has led to a process of marginalisation and exclusion which has attracted a great deal of attention.[2]

In these countries, as in the United States, where the unemployment rate remains low, there is an increased tendency towards aggressive behaviour and violence in the workplace, and above all an ever-more general feeling of insecurity.[3] This is expressed in opinion polls and lies at the heart of social debates in the United States, together with income inequalities which are becoming more acute to the extent that some people are paid wages which do not allow them or their families an adequate standard of living. The mass redundancies which accompanied the restructuring of large American enterprises are probably the immediate cause of this insecurity. Nevertheless, mobility, which has always been a distinctive feature in the United States, now appears to lead, in many cases, to jobs which are less well paid than previously. The method of labour protection, essentially based on collective enterprise agreements rather than on a labour code or its equivalent, strengthens still further this instability. Combined with an increase in the wage gap to the detriment of the least skilled workers, such instability gives rise to the polarisation of the workforce and jeopardises social integration. Moreover, analysts have noted the existence of a form of social exclusion which is spreading and which leads to unemployment, generation after generation, for members of certain ethnic minorities who may lose any kind of reference to work in their lives.

In Central and Eastern Europe, the new phenomenon of impoverishment now affects large sections of the population, including those in employment, while the problem remains endemic in a very large number of developing countries. The divide between the haves and the have-nots is also growing in this area.

From a historical point of view, governments have adopted three types of policy, at least in order to maintain or to restore sound social cohesion among their fellow citizens: enlightened despotism, laissez-faire and the practice of the Welfare State. In the eighteenth century, the Austrian Empire applied a policy of virtuous authoritarianism, which is a classic example of enlightened despotism. The powers that were made their own analysis of the problems encountered and imposed the remedies which they deemed to be appropriate. This *modus operandi* is close to that of certain current political leaders who, as brilliant technocrats, consider themselves to be in a privileged position to assess the difficulties of their peoples and to provide the necessary remedies.

The laissez-faire strategy adopted elsewhere is very different: the governments concerned leave the task of making the necessary adjustments, including in social affairs, to the "invisible hand" of the market.

Finally, the third policy has satisfied the desire expressed by citizens, particularly in Western Europe, to see the State establish rules, institutions or practices which place them out of reach of social risks. This policy is based on an accepted duty of solidarity and, more often than not, on an agreement, explicit or otherwise, between the large employers' and trade union confederations. In such cases, many authors have referred to the Welfare State or, in Germany, to the Social State.

However, in their modern form – and their implementation through legal standards and institutions – these three policies have not managed to reduce significantly the social divides referred to above. By contrast, such divides appear to be more pronounced than in the recent past. The modern forms of enlightened despotism have frequently blurred the divide between the public and the personal; this does not always correspond – and with good cause – to the needs and the desires of those that are governed; the risks of choosing the wrong policy are obvious. A laissez-faire approach has never guaranteed a minimum subsistence level for the most impoverished, especially during periods of constrained economic circumstances; in practice, different social assistance systems ("safety nets") have often rectified the brutal aspects of such a policy. Finally, criticism has converged on the Welfare State which has been considered too unwieldy in the face of the globalisation of the capital, commodity and labour markets; the survival of the Welfare State, without adjustment and in a context of the liberalisation of capital and commodity exchanges, would presuppose solidarity between States, which does not really exist. In short, if it wishes to retain a role in devising and implementing social policies, the State must reform itself.

Currently, income disparities and the loss of power of the traditional social actors give rise to the fear that solidarity will break down and society will break up into two categories, those of the haves and the have-nots, which would come to replace the classes prevalent under the *Ancien Régime*.

Of significance is the fact that the term "social" in the expression "social question" has undergone a change in meaning. Historically speaking, it referred to the division between the social classes and, in particular, to the proletarian working class in its relations with the dominant and wealthy bourgeoisie.[4] Solidarity, as it developed at the time, was based on profession and class, and united those whose fate and risks were of a similar nature. At the end of the twentieth century, the system of social classes has substantially broken down in Europe, or at least the effects of this stratification no longer make themselves so strongly felt on the labour market. From this point of view, the situation has come to resemble the conditions prevalent in the United States and Japan. The social question currently faced by industrialised societies and indeed developing countries relates not to the impoverishment of workers, but of all those, be they employed or self-employed, who find themselves caught up, owing to their forced inactivity, their insufficient wages, or the uncertain nature of their employment, in a wave which either forces or keeps them outside the established structures.

2.2. A Greater Diversity of Social Players

In addition to the unsuccessful policies, there has been a significant weakening in the power of traditional social players. Even if this idea should not be exaggerated, the internationalisation of the market economy and its regionalisation, especially in Europe, inevitably reduce the possibilities for action by the public authorities, in particular in the social sphere. A Keynesian national policy presupposed complete State control over economic instruments. Such a policy can no longer operate in the same manner when Nations lose part of their authority. However, more than ever governments are called upon to act in response to the problems of employment and, in particular, social protection.[5]

Governments frequently turn to employers' and trade union associations for help. However, in exactly the same context these associations are faced with serious difficulties. The problems of trade unions are well known, since membership rates are falling in many countries. Employers' organisations are also undergoing a period of upheaval. Diversification and the fragmentation of interests on the one hand (the concerns of those with stable jobs obviously differ from those of the unemployed and workers in a precarious situation) and on the other (SMEs and multinationals can have widely differing interests) affect both types of associations to the extent that their respective monopolies on representation are challenged. Many enterprises, especially larger ones, seek to preserve their freedom of action in the field of personnel management. Nevertheless, they sometimes establish more or less informal networks between themselves. Industrial relations may be included in the meeting agendas of the chairmen and CEOs of the largest American firms or of the "business councils" set up elsewhere. The management of the main Japanese enterprises holds sectoral, intersectoral or industrial group coordination meetings, in particular in response to the famous spring offensives (*shunto*). From a trade union point of view, the fragmentation of interests undermines the traditional solidarity between workers. Furthermore, the group which is traditionally best placed with regard to trade union activity, i.e. regular salaried workers, is shrinking, while a large number of organisations of all kinds claim to represent interests which are at times very specific (consumers, the environment, women, ethnic minorities, local communities, the unemployed and so on), but which tally with those the trade unions wish to represent.

In short, both employers' associations and trade union federations have now to compete more with other groups as opposed to focusing on unity of action.

Among the phenomena witnessed is the increase in strength of new players on the world stage. Multinational enterprises are among the most prominent; a few (still small in number) do not even have any special links with particular countries and locate their headquarters where their major directors happen to be at a particular time. Regional groupings such as the European Union, MERCOSUR or NAFTA also feature among the new players. Non-governmental organisations (NGOs) have, for their part, and with the aid of new communication techniques, set up transnational networks whose influence is at times formidable.[6] All these players have adapted more quickly to the opening up of borders and to free trade than countries themselves have adapted to more rigid structures.

The reduction in the State's role reflects not only the increased importance attached to international players. Activities are also increasing at local and municipal levels. There also, the initiatives taken by NGOs modify the shape of societies. More and more public authorities are entrusting them with the tasks that they are no longer able or wish to undertake, thereby setting in motion a privatisation process which does not involve the commercial sector but, nevertheless, releases them of certain responsibilities. Similarly, there is an ever increasing number of activities launched by institutions at levels below that of the State. The majority of American federal States have an official observer to the World Trade Organisation. The German *Länder*, the Belgian linguistic communities or the British local authorities send representatives to the European Union. The Rhône-Alpes region of France has established direct relations with Geneva and Turin, with a view to solving cross-border-related problems such as that of seasonal workers.

Borders are therefore becoming more fluid and less dissuasive. Some begin to dream of a situation, on a world level, similar to that which prevailed in Western Europe in the seventeenth or even eighteenth century, when Nations did not have such a clearly established identity as they did subsequently. Travellers' notes show that they were able to move around without facing any particular administrative difficulties up to the very edge of the Ottoman Empire. This type of relation presupposes a certain community of views and interests. It may also be stated fairly definitely that following the fall of the communist regimes in Russia and neighbouring countries, on a world level, there is greater convergence in individual views of the organisation of production and labour.

3. A Decent Work Policy

To have decent work is still the primary means for most people to ensure a minimum income security. The concept of decent work addresses issues such as workers' protection and production systems, the links between the quality and quantity of work, and between rights and development. The notion and substance of decent work vary with economic and social structures, stages of economic progress and different institutional frameworks. The attainment of decent work is also dependent upon appropriate macroeconomic and other public policies; and coherent action by the international community to integrate social and economic objectives.[7]

Such a broad approach is necessary to support a more coherent global dialogue to achieve integrated policies within the national societies and the international community for economic and social development. However, it raises the question of the ways and means to elaborate a decent work paradigm. I would like to propose hereafter some elements for that discussion.

3.1. Three Categories of Standards

Classifying labour standards in three groups, as can be done for ILO standards,[8] enables progress to be made in a discussion of how such standards assist in shaping a new social system to be more responsive to present problems. The first group relates to the fundamental rights of men and women at work; the second covers the rules of a promotional or programmatic character; and the third relates to the more technical provisions of the labour and social security laws which form the crux of current debates.

In most countries, the standards of the first category can be found in the constitutional provisions dealing with public freedoms or social rights. They relate to freedom of association and collective bargaining, the abolition of child labour and forced labour, and to equality of employment opportunities and treatment. Everyone recognises their essential nature and international instruments have accorded them a clearly dominant role.

This is the case with regard to the United Nations Covenant on Civil and Political Rights and, above all, the Covenant on Economic, Social and Cultural Rights. It is the case with the ILO Constitution, several ILO Conventions and the Declaration on Fundamental Principles and Rights at Work and its Follow-up, adopted in June 1998 by the International Labour Conference. It should be emphasised that, although this text is essentially directed at the Member States of the Organisation, it nevertheless constitutes a solid basis for going beyond the purely inter-State nature of the conventional international instruments. The Declaration focuses on the essential social rights I have just mentioned and, even in this regard, is limited to succinct provisions, without providing details of the means for implementing them. Its cogency remains limited and the follow-up procedures are clearly less demanding than the traditional ILO supervisory mechanisms. Consequently, although the Declaration is directed primarily at the Member States, which are invited to take implementing measures, it can easily serve, by virtue of the general nature of its statement, as a direct reference for the new players on the world stage.

The Declaration can be used to define the rules to be followed, common to the ILO and the large international financial institutions, in their activities at country level. It may be echoed in the social charters adopted by regional bodies such as the European Union, Council of Europe, NAFTA and MERCOSUR in particular; more often than not, such charters are largely based on the ILO standards. Moreover, the Declaration can be invoked by NGOs demanding the establishment of a list of basic principles to be respected in relation to social policies; it may serve as inspiration to multinational enterprises when they draft their codes of social conduct or define the criteria to be respected in their so-called social relations or their social audits. Consequently, private initiatives help to complement national law on these different points or, more frequently, to ensure greater respect for them.

The second category of standards covers provisions which are more programmatic or promotional than directly compulsory. They aim to translate into laws the social policies of a government, especially in fields such as employment, vocational training or the fight against discrimination. They seek to make the activities of the authorities in these areas more coherent and more systematic; they set aims to be achieved, establish appropriate mechanisms and structures for the programmes chosen and, where necessary, specify measures on the labour market and the means of evaluating the effectiveness of such measures. With regard to employment, for example, some of these measures appear to be directed more towards the immediate future (for example, exemptions from social charges to boost the recruitment of young people at a particular time), while others are designed to provide the basis for a strategy to combat unemployment (such as the reorganisation of the system of vocational training or, in more simple terms, incentives to encourage geographical or professional mobility).

These standards are general and flexible in their wording, and serve essentially as incentives; their implementation requires the adoption of very diverse measures. These provisions do not place any immediate obligation on an employer or other person, but contain an obligation of means, i.e. conducting certain activities, devising or implementing certain projects, working towards certain objectives and so on. It should, however, be noted that directly compulsory provisions can co-exist in the same law with these programmatic standards. Legislation on equality of opportunity and treatment provides numerous illustrations of this: in addition to promotion schemes, other rules render void acts of discrimination committed in the area under consideration.

A good illustration of programmatic standards comes from Japan where legislation contains obligations "for individuals to do their utmost" to take such and such a measure, as opposed to placing an obligation on someone. It is then the responsibility of the administrative authorities – in most cases the Ministry of Labour – frequently with the trade unions to persuade enterprises to do all they can to translate into reality the spirit of the legislation.

In 1986 for example, an amendment to the Japanese Law on Employment Stability for the Elderly requested enterprise heads to "do their utmost" to extend the compulsory retirement age at least to 60 (until that time, it was much lower). A further amendment was made in 1990, which placed the obligation on employers to "do their utmost" to re-employ retirees who so desired until the age of 65. On this basis, the Ministry of Labour ordered action programmes to be drawn up. Nevertheless, the government subsequently considered it necessary to increase the impact of the measures taken and on that occasion, in 1994, made it compulsory to retire at the age of 60: the law also strengthened the powers of incentive of civil servants so that enterprise heads retained their staff until they reached the age of 65.[9] Although the policy of extending the age up to which people are allowed to work can vary owing to current economic difficulties, the technique used appears to be deeply enshrined in the country's legal tradition.

Programmatic standards give rise to little debate. They are generally well accepted, apart from in cases where they make more severe the administrative constraints placed on enterprises. Moreover, sufficient use has not been made of the means they offer to overcome differences of opinion and to devise modern social policies on certain important subjects, such as the reform of working hours.

The majority of labour standards belong to a third group whose technical content is more specific. They pertain to working conditions, legal procedures and labour administration. Those relating to social security may also be added. This is the area in which most of the debates on the future of the legal protection of labour arise. National and international legislators are confronted by contradictory objectives, tensions between the competing concerns of enterprise heads and salaried workers, or even other groups, and the need to ensure that these concerns satisfy the general interest. Choices must be made. At times, these choices are the result of more or less official negotiations and mutual concessions; on other occasions, they are the result of delicate arbitration procedures. Often in democratic societies, legislative authorities seek this minimum consensus which represents a guarantee of the effectiveness of standards.

Agreement is reached more easily on a subject such as health and safety at work than on others. Employers and workers largely share the same concerns in this area, which are generally linked to technical changes, even if their views differ on the methods of practical application or the speed of the reforms envisaged. It is no surprise, for example, that many European standards exist in relation to this question. A joint approach is much more difficult to achieve on subjects where supporters of rigidity and defenders of flexibility differ in their opinions. Working time is a striking example of this. Controversy is still rife on the manner in which the old international rules on the number of hours worked should be adapted to new technical constraints and social aspirations. It should be emphasised that deadlock is not reached in most cases as a result of bureaucratic perspectives or a lack of flexibility in the national system: they relate more to the difficulty of reconciling varied and differing points of view on complex and important issues. For many years, for example, the lifting of the prohibition on night work for women in industry divided employers and employees alike. Solutions are now to be found in most European labour laws. It is also true that European Union bodies have made great efforts to achieve such solutions.

This type of agreement on the basic principles of regulations is more often lacking these days; as a result, whole areas of labour law are brought into question. Furthermore, a compromise appears to be all the more difficult to achieve since trade union and even employers' confederations are themselves experiencing more difficulties than in the past in speaking out on behalf of all those they represent. Consequently, the future of this branch of the law requires an adjustment of the mechanisms designed to achieve social consensus (B) which enables the balance between economic constraints and labour protection (C) to be redefined in a stable manner.

3.2. *A Possible Reshaping of "Industrial" Relations*

A return to the principles of freedom and democracy, on which modern societies are founded, helps to find ways to overcome the present difficulties. The freedoms of association, expression and assembly certainly provide all those who encounter common problems with the opportunity to form intermediate institutions between citizens and the State. In France, reference has been made to a real "boom" in the social sector of associations.[10] Three types of groups in particular have assumed real significance:[11] employers' and workers' organisations, social associations and other NGOs with social aims.

The first group corresponds to actual employers' and workers' organisations, even if their structures sometimes differ from those of traditional trade unions and business associations. It should be recalled that the concept of workers' or employers' organisations used by the ILO[12] is broad in scope and refers to all organisations designed to promote and defend the interests of such workers or employers. Consequently, this concept encompasses, for example, movements supporting the weakest sections of the working population, including home workers or those employed in the informal sector in developing countries in Africa, Latin America or Asia (e.g. in India). It now appears to be received wisdom[13] that these new forces, which have proved they have staying power, can be combined with trade union action by using the possibilities offered by networking or, more simply, that better coordination with important social movements is supported. At times, there is, however, a lot to be learned from their methods of action which are often less standardised and more individualised, since they place greater emphasis on personal initiative and responsibility.

Other private groupings, in particular those which have established a regional or global structure, have recently had a visible impact on social, national or international policies. However, their activities often remain irregular or unforeseeable, linked as they are to the media coverage they receive and to financial sponsorships. By contrast, owing to their permanent and truly representative nature (even when only 5 to 10 per cent of the working population are members, their rate of affiliation is normally clearly higher than that of the other groups), trade unions are unshakeable pillars of the social landscape. Two other types of groups should be distinguished here.

A second group brings together organisations which pursue social aims but which were set up with different objectives: the promotion and protection of women, consumers, the environment, small shopkeepers, civil liberties, local or neighbourhood interests, students, parents of pupils, community or ethnic minority concerns and so on; some are in the form of a cooperative. All such groupings act as intermediary bodies between their members and the authorities. Several features of employers' and workers' organisations can also be found in the democratic process of their creation

21

(by association) and decision-making; this process generally ensures that their structures are transparent and enables their representative nature and objectives to be easily verified. Consequently, relations built on greater trust can therefore be formed between these groupings, and between them and trade union or employers' confederations. In practice, there is an ever-increasing number of alliances which are concluded for protest campaigns or for other aims.

The third group of non-governmental organisations with social aims is not, at least in essential terms, based on associative principles. These organisations include various institutions ranging from churches, charitable undertakings and support networks (in particular for the unemployed) to technical cooperation projects, development assistance or the protection of health and safety at work. These institutions are served by men and women on the ground, for example, who work on an individual basis to train, integrate and reintegrate those facing social exclusion (the long-term unemployed, homeless, beneficiaries of social assistance or a minimum guaranteed income, heavily indebted households, illegal immigrants, drug addicts or, quite simply, the impoverished). These institutions frequently operate in cooperation with the local authorities, their development agents and social workers. The absence of the same transparency in terms of representation and origin of resources at times makes joint projects with the latter category of groups more problematic. Nevertheless, on occasions they have also proved to be useful partners.

It should be considered whether these partnerships, especially between those founded on associative principles, could expand the basis of the social consensus at a time when the State is expected less to play the role of guarantor than that of a driving force and mediator which creates an environment designed to enhance dialogue. In particular, central authorities are called upon to create the institutions and channels of communication which facilitate such consultation.[14] It may be necessary to incorporate these representative players in the institutions which implement social policies for the purposes of vocational training, funding, social security and so on, to extend the scope of their free negotiations, or also to make them participate as a matter of course in the preparation of social policies and of the laws which translate such policies into sustainable measures which are, to varying degrees, compulsory.

The expansion of the basis of the social contract concluded between the different population groups should enable the vast majority of interests involved to be covered and make it possible to go beyond the sole concerns – which are sometimes considered to be "corporatist" – of more restricted groups. A permanent dialogue, with all the social categories involving their representatives, should enable the links between these various interests to be better guaranteed than they are currently and allow participation in a true reorganisation of life in society. This will provide a more consensus-based manner of attempting to define the general interest. This also demonstrates an important aspect of development which labour law can be expected to provide: organising these institutions and new or transformed relations on a legal basis; setting the framework and the guiding principles thereof, guaranteeing that they will survive the risks generated by chance events, but making them sufficiently flexible so that the creativity of the social players is not constrained.

In order for them to be effective, these institutions and relations must exist at all levels where dialogue can be conducted. Exchanges have traditionally taken place at national level, and within sectors of activity or enterprise, whereby attention has been focused on one or the other, according to the countries and periods in question.

The opening up of borders to capital and commodities, and to economic globalisation, and in the first place its regionalisation, have made the need to guarantee collective labour relationships at these levels obvious. The pioneering role played by the European Union in this regard is well known,[15] in particular with the establishment of European Works Councils and the conclusion of collective labour agreements at multinational level (for example Danone), within sectors of activity such as footwear, or at the inter-sectoral level (with collective agreements on parental leave, part-time work and fixed-term employment). However, initiatives taken elsewhere are also worthy of attention. Thus, the Japanese have set up a conference – which is held twice a year – to liaise on multinational labour problems. This conference led to the publication, by the Association of Japanese Overseas Companies, of a code of voluntary conduct for national investors abroad. Enterprises such as Honda or Matsushita have established transnational relations for the purposes of cooperating with trade unions as part of their human resources development strategy.

Negotiating levels must also be expanded to the local level. A significant number of successful experiments and arrangements put in place at this level can already be cited. This is the case in Italy with the organisation of timetables – at work, on public transport, and for private and public services – in several large towns and cities. Associations of women, users, shopkeepers, neighbours and so on have joined forces with the trade unions and public authorities (and sometimes also with employers' organisations) so as to give greater expression to citizens' demands in professional and public life.[16] This is the case with regard to the Garment Industry Corporation, a tripartite organisation set up in New York in order to protect the textile industry and employment in this sector, by improving qualifications and marketing methods, and through the use of new production and management techniques.[17] This is the case with regard to local employment initiatives which have proved to be a success in Belgium and Ireland.[18]

On each occasion, the role of the State, and of the law, will consist in recognising these players, promoting their development (by eliminating the obstacles including, discriminatory practices), recognising the institutions which they set up (by participating, for example, in their establishment) and in facilitating relations between them. This task assumes a particular dimension with regard to specific types of activities, such as those in the informal sector or involving SMEs, where it is more difficult to establish actual consultations on social issues. Here also, however, there are examples of successful attempts to put in place a suitable framework. The successes achieved in the districts of Emilia Romagna in Italy are an example of such projects which are often studied.[19] Even in the informal sector, success is quite common.[20]

It should also be noted that the State and its legal arm must not only promote these renewed forms of participation, they must also guarantee sound coordination between the different levels.

For what type of agreements is this renewed dialogue intended? Irrespective of whether they are eventually translated into laws, collective agreements or a combination of a framework law and implementing conventions, these agreements should relate above all, while employment remains hard to come by or precarious, to the fight against unemployment and income insecurity, and against the increased inequalities and risks of seeing the divide between the haves and have-nots broaden. In other words, the content of the provisions contained in these social covenants which belong to a new generation would be less regulatory than programmatic, would relate to obligations regarding means rather than results and would primarily, according to the Japanese formula, require everyone to do their utmost, while remaining flexible as to the choice of the methods used. Penalties could be reserved for cases of inaction and for those where the mechanics of a consensus would grind to a halt and where abuses would be committed.

Certain formulae have already been proposed, whereby possible career paths have been traced consisting of modules to be arranged and alternating working time, retraining time and periods of leave (maternity, parental, military service and so on).[21] Better qualifications and increased independence – which go hand in hand – would enable different individual activities to be coordinated in a more satisfactory manner – professional labour, training and retraining, periods of leave for a particular purpose, voluntary or poorly remunerated tasks but which have a high social value (looking after children or the elderly, assistance to victims of all kinds of violence and so on) – and would allow these types of work to be planned for the whole of a person's life. Such provisions would make it easier to find a compromise between opposing interests, firstly for workers themselves and then within their industrial relations; thus, a satisfactory balance between private (family) life and professional activities could be sought.

Lastly, at the macroeconomic policy level, such provisions could enable acceptable compromises to be found, balancing sometimes contradictory factors: security and mobility on the labour market through social insurance measures which, whilst compulsory, encourage the beneficiary to be proactive rather than to rely on assistance; a necessary centralisation of solidarity programmes, but recognition of the benefits offered by local structures in terms of new ideas and new initiatives; encouraging the hiring of workers while maintaining genuine equality of opportunity and treatment; minimum assistance to associations involved in the defence of disadvantaged groups, but the will, as one finds already, to stand at their side; in other words to help them to help themselves and to let them take their destiny into their own hands, rather than showing them the way.[22]

3.3. *The Effects of Protective Standards on the Running of Enterprises and Beyond*

The ideas expressed thus far have focused on the most realistic and most effective method of adapting the protection necessary for workers to a changing economic environment. These ideas are similar to those of authors[23] who refuse to assimilate economic liberalisation with deregulation and emphasise that new rules must be created if the new international markets are to function properly. In particular, new social standards must enable individuals to manage the uncertainties created by these markets.

More than ever it should be recalled, however, that since they were first introduced legal labour rules have also been tied to economic concerns, and that they have related not to a workers' law but to an employment law, i.e. the organisation of production activity. In other words, the constraints and capabilities of the labour market must remain at the centre of the measures taken.[24]

Obvious confusion reigns in the debates devoted to the economic advantages and shortcomings of certain labour rules or forms of regulation. The fact that these discussions and disputes involve experts from varying disciplines – sociologists, political analysts, philosophers and many others, in addition to legal experts and economists – adds to the sense of disorder.

Adapting or revising a labour standard consists essentially in giving legal form to a particular social policy, which is required to correspond to a given situation and, often, to differing concerns of an economic, political, cultural and professional nature. Faced with this series of factors, a legislative authority chooses a solution which seeks in principle to reconcile, at least to a partial extent, the interests concerned. The fact remains that the economic impact of the rule envisaged is a determining factor in the decision-making process.

This effect should also be evaluated in a relatively precise manner. The method used is either quantitative or qualitative. Most of the authors who have broached this task have, very broadly speaking, chosen the second option.[25] Many have advocated a "high road" for the development of enterprises and national economies, i.e. the option of satisfactory protection for employment and labour which provides a comparative advantage in terms of motivation and productivity. The argument appears to be convincing, but it does not put an end to the debate. Moreover, both in Europe and Japan where this phenomenon was previously limited, there is a noticeable increase in the recruitment of workers on a casual basis, thereby avoiding the financial risks of without-limit-of-time appointments.

Consequently, there appears to be an expectation that an exact measurement will be provided in an area where it appears to be impossible to arrive at such certainties. How therefore can the precise economic effect of protective provisions be determined? However, owing to a lack of data and figures, the fear persists, albeit diffuse and in many respects irrational, that a limited notice period, prior to the end of an employment contract, can endanger the competitiveness of enterprises.

In the circumstances, recourse to economic indicators on the impact of labour standards appears to be the best possible method. On occasions, a law has assumed this influence. Thus, Belgian legislation on employment promotion and the "preventive" safeguarding of productivity has limited wage increases negotiated collectively according to a complex system, but which takes into account the changes in wage costs in Germany, France and the Netherlands, neighbouring States which are considered to be the major competitors.

It is scarcely necessary to emphasise the importance of the definition and selection of the elements used to compile the above indicators. To reconsider the example of redundancy legislation, how can it be explained that recent analyses of the economic effects of such legislation excluded Japan – where the dismissal of a worker creates a particular sense of unease – while its economy grew in spectacular fashion in the 1980s? A clear distinction should again be made between macro, meso and microeconomic levels. Legislation on the prevention of and compensation for industrial accidents, a further example, imposes certain costs on enterprises: it can, however, enable them to make greater savings. Nevertheless, the effects of these legal provisions on the national accounts are still clearly more positive.[26]

* * *

The idea of establishing social policy and labour regulations was based on several different pillars which are to be found in the preparation of national legislation and ILO standards. The first and most important is obviously the pursuit of social justice and the elimination of unacceptable employment conditions. Furthermore, such conditions would be likely – the second pillar – to cause serious disturbances and to endanger the social and political stability of a country. We have seen recent examples of this phenomenon. The fear of economic competition and of a loss of competitiveness is the third pillar: in cases where certain enterprises do not respect a decent system of labour, the others might be reluctant to do so in order not to increase their costs. From this point of view, the adoption of uniform and compulsory rules for all constitutes a guarantee against those who would seek to benefit, in the face of fierce competition, from poor working conditions.

These reasons still exist today: the opening of borders and markets has even increased the regional or global dimension of these concerns. A "decent work" policy must always cover such concerns, strike a balance between contradictory pressures and, finally, offer real security to all the parties concerned: to workers, be they employed or self-employed, who fear for their jobs or incomes; to enterprise heads who ensure that a company runs smoothly and is answerable to all those who have invested in it; and also, to the public authorities, each of which is responsible, at its own level, for maintaining or restoring sound social cohesion of which work remains, irrespective of its desirability, the best guarantee.

Bibliography

D. Andreoni, *Le coût des accidents du travail et des maladies professionnelles*, Geneva, ILO, 1985.

R. Andreotti, *Sindacato e politiche dei tempi in Italia*, Geneva, International Institute for Labour Studies, internal document, 1998.

R. Blanpain, *Institutional Changes and European Social Policies after the Treaty of Amsterdam*, The Hague, Kluwer, 1998.

R. Blanpain, "Social dialogue. Economic interdependence and labour law", Report to the 6th European Congress for Labour Law and Social Security (Warsaw, 13–17 September 1999), Warsaw, Scholar, 1999.

R. Blanpain (ed.), "Multinational enterprises and the social challenges of the XXIst century", in *Bulletin of Comparative Labour Relations*, No. 37, The Hague, Kluwer, 2000.

R. Castel, *Les métamorphoses de la question sociale, une chronique du salariat*, Paris, Fayard, 1995.

R. Castel, "Centralité du travail et cohésion sociale", in J. Kergoat, J. Boutet, H. Jacot, D. Linhart, *Le Monde du travail*, Paris, La Découverte, 1998.

Commissariat Général du Plan, *Le travail dans vingt ans*, Paris, O. Jacob, 1995, *La documentation française*.

F. Cossentino, F. Pyke, W. Sengenberger, *Local and regional response to global pressure: The case of Italy and its industrial districts*, Geneva, International Institute for Labour Studies, 1996.

F. Durán López, "Globalización y relaciones de trabajo", in *Civitas*, No. 32, Nov.-Dec, 1998.

J.B. Figueiredo, A. de Haan, *Social exclusion: An ILO perspective*, Geneva, International Institute for Labour Studies, 1998.

R. Freeman, J.L. Medoff, *What do unions do*, New York, Basic Books, 1984.

M. Geddes, *Local partnership: A successful strategy for social cohesion?* Dublin, European Foundation for the Improvement of Living and Working Conditions, 1998.

B.G. Herman, *See what? The New York apparel industry in the global economy: Inevitable decline or possibilities for industrial upgrade?* Working document (International workshop on global production and local jobs: New perspectives on enterprise networks, employment and local development policy, Geneva, 9–10 March 1998), International Institute for Labour Studies, Geneva, 1998.

ICFTU, *The global market: Trade unionism's greatest challenge*, 16th World Congress of the ICFTU, Brussels, 25–29 June 1996, Brussels, 1996.

ILO, *World Labour Report*, Geneva, ILO, 1995.

ILO, *World Labour Report 1997–98*, "Industrial Relations, democracy and social stability", Geneva, 1997.

ILO, *Decent Work*. Report of the Director-General to the 87th Session (June 1999) of the International Labour Conference, Geneva, ILO, 1999.

C.W. Jenks, *Law, freedom and welfare*, London, Oceana Publications, 1963.

Labour Law and Industrial Relations at the Turn of the Century, Liber emicorum in honour of Prof. Dr. Roger Blanpain, The Hague, Kluwer, 1998.

K.L. Ladear, "Social risks, welfare rights and the paradigms of proceduralisation. The combining of the liberal constitutional State", in J. de Munck, J. Lenoble, M. Molistz (eds.), *L'avenir de la concertation sociale en Europe*, Louvain, Centre for the Philosophy of Law, Catholic University of Louvain, 1995.

A. Lalande, *Vocabulaire technique et critique de la philosophie*, Paris, PUF, 1962.

B. Langille, "The ILO and the new economy: Recent developments", in *The International Journal of Comparative Labour Law and Industrial Relations*, Vol. 15, Autumn, 1999.

G. Malaurie, "Le boom des associations", in *Problèmes économiques*, No. 2605, 24 Feb. 1999.

J.T. Matthews, "Power shift" in *Foreign Affairs*, Jan.-Feb. 1997.

OECD (Labour Management Programme), *The role of trade unions in local development*, Paris, 1997.

F. Pyke, G. Becattini, W. Sengenberger (eds.), *Industrial districts and inter-firm cooperation in Italy*, Geneva, International Institute for Labour Studies, 1990.

G. Rodgers, Ch. Gore, J.B. Figueiredo (eds.), *Social exclusion: Rhetoric, reality, responses*, Geneva, International Institute for Labour Studies, 1995.

W. Sengenberger, D. Campbell (eds.), *Creating economic opportunities. The role of labour standards in industrial restructuring*, Geneva, International Institute for Labour Studies, 1994.

J.M. Servais, "Le droit international en mouvement: déploiement et approches nouvelles", in *Droit social*, No. 5, May 1991.

J.M. Servais, "International labour organization", in R. Blanpain (ed.), *International Encyclopaedia of Laws*, The Hague, Kluwer, 1996.

J.M. Servais, *Droit en synergie sur le travail. Eléments de droit international et comparé du travail*, Bruyelles, Bruylant, 1997.

W. Streeck, "The Internationalization of Industrial Relations in Europe: Prospects and Problems", in *Politics and Society*, Vol. 26, No. 4, Dec. 1998.

A. Supiot (ed.), *Le travail en perspectives*, Paris, LGDJ, 1998.

– (ed.), *Au-delà de l'emploi. Transformations du travail et devenir du droit du travail en Europe*, Paris, Flammarion, 1999.

A. Valli (ed.), *Tempo di lavoro e occupazione. Il caso italiano*, Rome, La Nuova Italia Scientifica, 1988.

NOTES

1   *World Labour Report 1997–98*: "Industrial relations, democracy and social stability", ILO, Geneva, 1997.

2   G. Rodgers, Ch. Gore, J.B. Figueiredo (eds.), *Social exclusion: Rhetoric, reality, responses*, Geneva, International Institute for Labour Studies, 1995; J.B. Figueiredo and A. de Haan, *Social exclusion: An ILO perspective*, Geneva, International Institute for Labour Studies, 1998. See also R.Castel, *Les métamorphoses de la question sociale, une chronique du salariat*. Paris, Fayard 1995, and "Centralité du travail et cohésion sociale, in J. Kergoat, J. Boutet, H. Jacot and D. Linhart, *Le Monde du travail*, Paris, La Découverte, 1998; A. Supiot (ed.), *Le travail en perspectives*, Paris, LGDJ, 1998.

3   ILO: *World Labour Report 1997–98*, "Industrial Relations, democracy and social stability", Geneva, 1997, p.116.

4   See for example A. Lalande, *Vocabulaire technique et critique de la philosophie*, Paris PUF, 1962, p. 998.

5   See *Labour Law and Industrial Relations at the Turn of the Century. Liber emicorum in honour of Prof. Dr. Roger Blanpain*, The Hague, Kluwer, 1998.

6   See J.T. Matthews, "Power shift" *Foreign Affairs*, January-February 1997, pp. 50–66.

7   See *Decent work*. Report of the Director-General to the 87th Session (June 1999) of the International Labour Conference, Geneva, ILO, 1999.

8   See J.M. Servais: "Le droit international en mouvement: déploiement et approches nouvelles", in *Droit social*, May 1991, No. 5, pp. 449ff; Comp. C.W. Jenks: *Law, freedom and welfare*, London, Oceana Publications, 1963, p. 103.

9   See ILO: *World Labour Report*, Geneva, 1995, pp. 27–28.

10 G. Malaurie: "Le boom des associations", *Problèmes économiques*, No. 2605, 24 February 1999, pp. 22ff.

11 ILO: *World Labour Report 1997–98*, "Industrial Relations, democracy and social stability", op.cit., pp. 47ff.

12 In particular in Convention No. 87 on the Freedom of Association and Protection of the Right to Organize, 1948, Convention No. 98 on the Right to Organize and Collective Bargaining, 1949, and Convention No. 141 on Rural Workers' Organizations, 1975.

13 See ICFTU: The global market: Trade unionism's greatest challenge, 16th World Congress of the ICFTU, Brussels, 25–29 June 1996, Brussels, 1996, p. 81.

14 See A. Supiot (ed.): *Au-delà de l'emploi. Transformations du travail et devenir du droit du travail en Europe*, Paris, Flammarion, 1999, especially paras. 586ff.; see also F. Durán López, "Globalización y relaciones de trabajo", *Civitas*, No. 32, Nov.–Dec. 1998, pp. 869–888.

15 See for example ILO: op.cit., pp. 37ff., 230 and 231.

16 See R. Andreotti: *Sindacato e politiche dei tempi in Italia*, Geneva, International Institute for Labour Studies, internal document, 1998.

17 B.G. Herman: *See what? The New York apparel industry in the global economy: Inevitable decline or possibilities for industrial upgrade?* Working document (International workshop on global production and local jobs: New perspectives on enterprise networks, employment and local development policy, Geneva, 9–10 March 1998), International Institute for Labour Studies, Geneva, 1998.

18 OECD (Labour Management Programme): *The role of trade unions in local development*, Paris, 1997; M. Geddes: *Local partnership: A successful strategy for social cohesion?* Dublin, European Foundation for the improvement of living and working conditions, 1998.

19   F. Pyke, G. Becattini, W. Sengenberger (eds.): *Industrial districts and inter-firm cooperation in Italy*, Geneva, International Institute for Labour Studies, 1990; F. Cossentino, F. Pyke, W. Sengenberger: *Local and regional response to global pressure: The case of Italy and its industrial districts*, Geneva, International Institute for Labour Studies, 1996.

20   ILO: op.cit., pp.175ff.

21   See the report of the Commission (Commissariat Général du Plan) headed by Jean Boissonnat: "Le travail dans vingt ans", Paris, O. Jacob, *La documentation française*, 1995; see also A. Valli (ed.): *Tempo di lavoro e occupazione. Il caso italiano*, Rome, La Nuova Italia Scientifica, 1988, pp. 13–38 and 177–197; K.L. Ladear: "Social risks, welfare rights and the paradigms of proceduralisation. The combining of the liberal constitutional State", in J. de Munck, J. Lenoble and M. Molistz (eds.): *L'avenir de la concertation sociale en Europe*, Louvain, Centre for the Philosophy of Law, Catholic University of Louvain, 1995, p.143.

22   ILO: op.cit., pp.230–231.

23   See for example W. Streeck: "The Internationalization of Industrial Relations in Europe: Prospects and Problems", in *Politics and Society*, Vol. 26, No. 4, December 1998, pp. 432–433.

24   See recently Br. Langille: "The ILO and the new economy: Recent developments", in *The International Journal of Comparative Labour Law and Industrial Relations*, Vol. 15, Autumn 1999, pp. 234–.

25   A large amount of literature exists on this subject, but the following are always worth looking back at, for example: R. Freeman and J.L. Medoff: "What do unions do", New York, *Basic books*, 1984, or W. Sengenberger and D. Campbell (eds.): *Creating economic opportunities. The role of labour standards in industrial restructuring*, Geneva, International Institute for Labour Studies, 1994.

26   D. Andreoni: *Le coût des accidents du travail et des maladies professionnelles*, Geneva, ILO, 1985.

Tayo Fashoyin

3. INDUSTRIAL RELATIONS IN DEVELOPING COUNTRIES[1]

1. INTRODUCTION

The pervasive feature of the industrial relations systems in the developing countries, as distinct from the industrialised countries, is that industrial relations policies in the former have, for the most part, been shaped by conditions of political and economic under-development. In situations such as this, the role of the state differs fundamentally from country to country. While market forces are often seen as the driving force of industrial relations in the industrialised market economies, the state in the developing countries is usually the chief architect of economic and social policies and exercises the overwhelming influence on industrial relations. As such, the role of the state, not simply as probably the largest employer, but also as the force behind economic, legal and institutional changes is a highly prominent one. Therefore, the worldwide changes that we are today witnessing through the forces of globalisation and liberalisation, and the accompanying national economic reforms, have created different sets of industrial relations responses from the actors developing countries.

This paper will briefly present an overview of the evolving industrial relations environment and the responses of the key actors in the developing countries. At the onset, it should be borne in mind that the routine description of certain countries as 'developing' in the 1960s is no longer a homogeneous configuration today. In fact, they fall into no less than two broad groups, based on comparative level of development. This broad grouping includes those countries that are referred to as the new industrialising countries of Asia, generally in Asia and includes South Korea, Singapore, Hong Kong and Taiwan and, in Africa, South Africa. The other group of countries, more or less referred to as the 'developing' or 'least developed' countries, includes Bangladesh in Asia, Bolivia in Latin America and Sierra Leone in Africa. However, despite the varying levels of development in the 'developing' countries as a whole, the industrial relations institutions and processes still share very common features.

R. Blanpain and C. Engels (eds), The ILO and the Social Challenge of the 21st Century, 31–43.
© 2001 *Kluwer Law International. Printed in Great Britain.*

1.1. Globalisation, Economic and Political Reforms

At the onset, we identify three interrelated forces which have fundamentally shaped industrial relations in the developing countries during the preceding two decades. These are economic reforms, political transformation and globalisation.

Most developing countries of Asia, Africa and Latin America underwent sweeping economic and political changes in the 1980s and 1990s. Economic reforms which marked a shift in development strategies away from import-substitution industrialisation and state-driven economies towards neo-liberal economic policies in which exports are prominent objectives are universal features of the economic reforms of the period. While reform policies vary from one country to another, they contain other common elements, including civil service reform designed to achieve cost-effectiveness, realistic approach to public spending, and overall curtailment of the role of the state in economic matters and corresponding commitment to private sector-led industrialisation As a result, the focus of reform has included the privatisation of previously extensive state enterprises, deregulation and trade liberalisation, by which prevailing state controls and interventions are replaced with market-oriented policies. In countries where these fundamental reforms have taken place, they have occurred within the context of adverse economic problems, such as high debts, high inflation and decline in standard of living. A commitment on the part of the state, often under external pressures, to reverse the unfavourable economic trend has inescapably led to the compromising of issues of the labour market. In turn this has aggravated social and labour problems and, in nearly all cases, has led to a curtailment of labour rights.

Most developing countries experienced fundamental political reforms, generally from various forms of authoritarian regime, to democratic rule during the 1980s and 1990s (Sandbrook, 1996). In a large proportion of developing countries, the trade union movement has played a significant role in the political transformation as support for authoritarian, one party or military rule crumbled during the democratisation campaign. In Latin America where generally political reforms appeared first in the 1980s, several countries, including Brazil, Argentina, Bolivia, Paraguay, Peru and Chile went through major constitutional reforms (Bronstein, 1995, ILO, 1999). In Africa, notable cases included South Africa which dismantled the notorious apartheid policy of separate development in 1994, and went through a democratic process to elect a majority government. In other countries of Southern Africa where autocratic or one party rule had prevailed in the post-independent period, e.g. Malawi, Mozambique, Tanzania and Zambia, neoliberal democracy was introduced (Fashoyin, 1998).

With few exceptions, fundamental political transformation occurred mainly in the 1990s in several Asian countries. For example, Nepal adopted a new constitution which introduced a monarchical democracy in which the right to assemble and the rights to freedom of expression and of association were recognised (Ratnam and Naidu, 1999). In Thailand and Indonesia, neoliberal political reforms were also introduced providing for constitutional changes, the most fundamental features of which include the recognition of the rights of workers to freely associate and to bargain collectively.

In this international onslaught on dictatorship, a major element in so far as industrial relations is concerned is the overwhelming support for the recognition of the fundamental rights of the workers at work, whether it concerns the right to organise into trade unions, or the right to effectively participate in decisions affecting the conditions of employment under which workers work. In those developing countries which have witnessed this resurgence of democracy, the effect on industrial relations institutions and processes has been very significant. Specifically, the changing political environment has afforded workers in a growing number of developing countries the ability to exercise their rights to form trade unions or to belong to one, and to actually see that such a right materialises.

The third external factor that has influenced the industrial relations environment is globalisation. Globalisation implies closer international integration of economic, political and social activities (IMF, 1997; Frenkel and Peetz, 1998). The internationalisation of markets has intensified financial, trade, technology and information exchanges, as well as other economic and social activities among countries. In the particular context of the labour market, new forms of employment, retrenchments and layoffs, the growth of foreign direct investments and export processing zones, and reduced collective bargaining have been the obvious consequences of globalisation. However, depending on the angle from which this phenomenon is viewed, it has its positive and negative effects on industrial relations.

For the developing countries, globalisation presents a dilemma. While it is assumed that globalisation will lead to interdependence which will accelerate worldwide convergence of employment relations, there is at present what can be seen as resistance in the developing world, towards this uniformity. In part this is due to the differences in the level of economic development, but more importantly because, in most cases, overall control by government of national economies is often very weak, creating as it does, differences in response to globalisation. Relatedly, there are marked differences in national and historical values, as well as the stability of labour market institutions. There is therefore hardly any doubt that the impact of this international phenomenon differs from one region to another, and indeed from one country to another. What is hardly questionable is the evidence that, by and large, the labour market institutions in the developing countries have had to bear a large brunt of the impact of globalisation.

2. CHANGING LABOUR MARKET, INSTITUTIONS AND POLICIES

2.1. *Informalisation of the Labour Market*

One of the noticeable and sweeping effects of the foregoing forces, particularly in the case of the developing countries has been on employment relations in the labour market. When economic reforms were introduced, massive retrenchment of workers followed, as a result of intensified public sector reform and privatisation. Some indication of the scale of this contraction of the labour market can be seen in the following proportion of the labour force in the informal economy (ILO, 1998):

Africa:	57.2 per cent
Latin America:	36.2 per cent
Asia:	32.8 per cent

In contrast, the size of the informal sector employment in Europe is given as 11.9 per cent. Arguably it is not that economic reform and globalisation have entirely been responsible for informalisation of labour. On the contrary, informal employment has for a long time been a characteristic feature of the labour market in the developing countries. All the same, the phenomenon has become more pronounced in the era of economic reform and liberalisation policies, both of which have brought about fundamental changes in employment.

Accompanying the growth of the informal economy in the developing countries is the notable emergence of the phenomenon referred to as contingent employment (ILO, 1998). New forms of employment, such as contract labour, outsourcing, flexitime, part-time work, etc. have appeared in various forms in the past decade or so. Unfortunately, in the case of the developing countries it is difficult to estimate or measure the proportion of the wage earning population engage in this form of employment. Nevertheless, contingent employment is a growing phenomenon in the developing countries as global competition intensifies in these countries. In so far as the developing countries are concerned, informal employment and contingent work are two sides of the same coin, particularly when we talk about the effect on industrial relations. On the one hand, neither development is a comfort to the trade union movement which has, in most cases, to face the complex and intractable organisational challenges that they bring about. On the other hand, these forms of employment introduce the additional problem of employment insecurity, and the broader issue of rights at work. In particular, they unavoidably reduce the scope of the collective bargaining machinery, which is the acclaimed instrument by which trade unions advance and protect the interest of their members.

2.2. Public Policy

One needs to observe further that in most developing countries, the labour market institutions are weak, in part as a result of the very structure of the economy and the labour market, in which wage employment is generally a small proportion of the labour force. In countries such as Pakistan, Indonesia, Sudan and Ethiopia, for example, wage employment in the formal sector represents a very small fraction of the labour force. Inescapably, institutions such as trade unions and employers are naturally weak. In the case of trade unions, their weakness often arises also from a public policy which is not totally supportive, particularly as to whether or not workers have the right to organise and to bargain. It is in this area that public policy changes have and will continue to have a remarkable effect, as part of neoliberal polices. Thus, accompanying democratisation is the increasing obligation to concede the rights of workers, and labour law reform has had the main characteristic of removing impediments on these rights to organise and bargain freely. The evolving public policy environment has had a dramatic effect on the behaviour of employers in these countries although, at the same time, globalisation has enabled some employers to implement employment policies whose net effect has been to undermine these labour rights.

Governments in developing countries, anxious to see that the fruits of globalisation do not elude their economies have tacitly joined the employers by introducing policies whose net effect has been the weakening of the trade unions (Frenkel and Peetz, 1998; Cook, 1998). In the particular case of the new industrialising states of East Asia, for example, the general response of governments to globalisation has been to protect investors by the design of polices which strengthens management control over industrial relations issues. Thus, in these countries and also in Africa and Latin America, public policy which on the one hand, provides for free and independent unions, as well as legal rights to bargaining have, on the other, provided practical constraints in the exercise of such rights. Restrictions on the scope of collective bargaining, on the issues for bargaining, and on the right to strike are practical problems inhibiting the exercise of workers' rights in these areas.

2.3. *Labour Law Reform*

In any event, accompanying economic and political reforms has been an equally fundamental reform of labour law, in a way that public policy has become more attuned to the emerging democratic society and, at the same time, seeking to meet the demands of the rapidly changing economic realities. In South Africa, labour rights were extended to all workers under the Labour Relations Act of 1995, and to Malawian workers through the Industrial and Labour Relations Act of 1996 (Fashoyin, 1998). In Nepal, the Industrial Relations Ordinance of 1992 recognised the right of workers to form legal unions and to bargain collectively. However, it should be borne in mind that some of the legislation that was made soon after political transformation was made primarily in response to political exigencies and were, in some cases, only barely sensitive to the demands of the evolving labour markets. This has thus raised a debate on the extent to which, in several countries, labour law reforms have taken account of the realities of production in these countries today. Central to this debate is the direction of labour law reform.

In attempting to understand the evolution of labour law reform in Latin America, observers have categorised the transformed of the labour codes into two groups (Bronstein, 1995; Cook, 1998). The transformation from restrictive dictatorial labour can thus be seen from two perspectives. The first are laws which are by their nature *protective*, in the sense that they have been introduced in response to the prevailing view that urgent and decisive legal framework ought to be in place so as to make

35

sharp break from the otherwise repressive polices of the authoritarian or dictatorial era. The Latin American countries that developed laws in this category include Brazil, Chile, Guatemala, Uruguay; South Africa and Malawi in Africa, and Indonesia, Nepal and Korea in Asia. Generally in most cases, the aim of the labour law reform was to restore the basic fundamental rights of works, including the right to organise and to bargain, fair and equitable wage found in minimum wage arrangements, define negotiable issues, such as extended working conditions, productivity improvement, workforce reduction, right to strike, right of the public service workers to organise and bargain, and so forth.

The second group of labour legislation can be described as *flexible*, in the sense that it is claimed that such orientation reflects a more realistic legal approach to addressing prevailing labour market and economic realities. Legislation of this type in the developing countries tends to give considerable freedom to employers, and is largely the basis for the introduction of various types of employment contract, decentralised bargaining, less stringent dismissal or retrenchment provisions, introducing performance related pay systems, flexible working hours and restricted overtime work, and less job security provisions. Some of the laws that were introduced in the post-dictatorial era have further been reviewed to achieve this goal. Countries such as Venezuela, Costa Rica, Columbia, Peru have undertaken this path (Bronstein, 1995; Cook, 1998). The industrial relations partners in Malawi, Nigeria, and South Africa are currently debating legislative reform along this direction.

It should be borne in mind that this categorisation is not a totally acceptable way to describe the evolving legal framework in the developing countries; nevertheless, it provides a view of the evolving public policy direction during the 1980s and 1990s. As might be expected, trade unions have generally hailed legislation which permits workers to exercise their fundamental rights and are critical of initiatives to review provisions that directly or covertly restrict or remove such rights. On the other hand, legislative framework which allows management a free-hand in setting certain employment conditions has been acclaimed as ideal for addressing global pressures, and for maintaining productivity and competitiveness.

Nonetheless, I find the categorisation just as useful for an understanding of the changing direction of public policy in the majority of African and Asian countries. However, it is evident that the two categories have not in the least resolved the debate over the proper direction of public policy. In fact, it seems obvious from the foregoing that the challenge remains on how the industrial relations community can develop middle of the road labour laws which accommodate the conflicting interests of industry. Thus, in-between these two categories are legislative reviews of a continuing nature, seeking to achieve what might be described as a 'proper' balance between on the one hand, the protection of worker' rights and, on the other, the enhancement of the ability of the employer to make optimal use of all human and non-human resources in order to effectively compete in global markets.

This process of continuing reform is taking place in most developing countries, in an effort to define a socially responsive labour policy. Yet, it would be inaccurate to suggest that middle of the road legislation has or will resolve the debate over the role of public policy in labour market regulation. Indeed, given that in several cases, much of the legislative changes that are taking place have not been fully discussed with the stakeholders, it becomes a matter of conjecture how a socially acceptable labour code can evolve from this approach. In fact, in a good number of cases, laws have been imposed by government, sometimes outside the normal industrial relations frame-work, and on the basis of external pressures and conditionalities of the international financial institutions.

2.4. *Trade Unions*

Trade unions were a major beneficiary of the neo-liberal political reforms of the 1980s and 1990s. Constitutional changes, accompanied in most cases by labour law reform sought to allow workers to form trade unions with less of the legal encumbrance that characterised the post independent era in most of the countries of Asia, Africa and Latin America. In Thailand where the right to organise and bargain was withdrawn from workers in state-owned enterprises, this right was restored by law as recently as 2000. It is true that, in general, the accompanying economic reform policies and globalisation have put unions on the defence in most countries, as a result of crushing economic conditions, and the social crisis occasioned at least in the short-term by these policies (Thomas, 1995). The effect of these environmental factors on the trade union movement across the developing countries has been noticeable structural and organisational changes (Ratnam and Naidu, 1999). There are a number of outstanding features of this development that can be mentioned.

Firstly, it has been stated earlier that there has been phenomenal contraction in employment in the formal sector where trade unions have traditionally recruited their members. Retrenchments in the wage sector have thus caused monumental decline in union membership in most developing countries. Secondly, it remains an issue of deep debate whether governments in the developing countries want to see strong unions. In many cases, as a result of tacit legislative and administrative designs, as well as internal union problems, trade unions in the developing countries have not achieved the unity they need to achieve a measure of cohesiveness. They are politically divided; and fragmentation or factionalisation of unions has occurred with great intensity. As a consequence, unions are too weak, both in organisational and leadership capacities to effectively assert their rights, or to negotiate at the workplace, the sectoral or national level.

Thirdly, structural changes in the labour market, both in terms of composition and also the growth of atypical employment: part-time, short-term, contract labour, etc. have undermined the role and influence of trade unions. These forms of employment are not conducive to unionisation. In other words, the new entrants into the labour market are too difficult for trade unions to organise. Fourthly, emergence of the human resource management approach, by which the employer deals with employees on an individual basis and invariably takes responsibility for much of the functions which a union would normally perform. Loyalty in a situation such as this is to the business and this reduces the appeal of the union. This has been accompanied by the reluctance of some new investors (FDIs) who are unwilling to support workers' organisation or to engage in bargaining.

Coupled with the foregoing obstacles to union development are some aspects of public policy initiatives taken as globalisation intensifies, the end result of which is the provision of legal or administrative restrictions on the freedom of workers to fully exercise their rights at work, particularly in the public service, and also in the export zones, agriculture, and in those sectors which are described as 'essential services'.

2.5. *Employers, and Employers' Associations*

In response to global competition and productivity, employers are also changing, both with respect to their organisational preferences and their industrial relations policies. Industrial restructuring, leading to lean production and substantial reduction in workforce, is taking place worldwide. Increasingly, several employers are reluctant to join employers associations, in favour of an individualistic approach to dealing with the consequences of globalisation which they argue affect various employers differently. The reluctance of employers to join has been particularly noticeable among the small-scale enterprises – which are growing and constitutes the majority of enterprises in the developing countries. The anxiety of this latter group of employers arises largely from the fear – which is probably not entirely misplaced – that bigger employers (often the multinationals) might use the employers' association to impose their will on the small-scale enterprises.

There are of course, exceptions to this lack of motivation for a concerted effort among employers (Fashoyin, 1998). Invariably, whether or not employers adopted a united front is strongly influenced by the experience they are facing in the product market. It is also a function of the relative strength of the trade unions. In Argentina, for example, the trade union movement has successfully asserted its influence in labour–management relations. Also in South Africa, the trade union movement which was a key actor in the struggle for popular democracy, is strong enough to resist unfettered powers of the employers. In any event, when employers unite to form an association, the employers' primary concern increasingly focuses on influencing the broader economic and public policy environment in favour of business. In so far as employment issues are concerned, these are becoming enterprise level focused, thereby enabling employers to adapt more speedily and appropriately to changing business environment. In recognition of this development the attention of several employers associations appear to focus on providing an efficient and effective institutional support system for their members to enable the latter to compete effectively in global markets. Examples of areas of this focus which are different from traditional industrial relations include information sharing, skills training and other employee development programme that strengthens the capacity of employers to adjust quickly to changing business situation.

3. Changing nature of Collective Bargaining

3.1. Decentralisation, Workplace Industrial Relations and Flexibility

The phenomena of globalisation, liberalisation and economic reform has had a great impact on collective bargaining and labour relations. Generally, collective bargaining in the developing countries depicts the following characteristics:

- reluctance of employers to bargain or, when they do, to bargain on narrowly defined issues.
- growing decentralisation of collective bargaining, with individual employers exercising more control over issues and processes of bargaining.
- preference among employers to discuss issues that are directly related to company performance, e.g. productivity, quality, safety and health, pay linked to performance.
- preference among employers to relate directly with their workers, without the intermediary of trade unions. This is the so-called human resource management approach.
- employment security is determined mainly by the dictates of global competition. Bearing this in mind, collective agreements tend to be of short duration.

As previously noted, the more evident impact of globalisation and economic reforms has been an increasing push for a greater role for management and workers at the enterprise level to enable them respond more quickly and appropriately to external pressures. In several developing countries, the push towards decentralisation of bargaining by employers is practically the only option available to trade unions for a meaningful collective bargaining to take place. Bearing in mind that trade unions are poorly organised, it happens that a test of their strength, in many countries, is at the enterprise level. On the other hand, and precisely for the same reasons, decentralisation or negotiation at the level of the enterprise is inhibiting the effectiveness of collective bargaining, partly because of management control of workplace relations, and partly because of the capacity problems in the union at the enterprise level.

In several countries across the developing world, policies which favour decentralisation and enterprise level bargaining have had the outstanding effect of weakening the union influence and the corresponding enhancement of management control. As might be expected, in most countries collective agreements have tended to be of short duration, often not lasting more than a year, undoubtedly because of rapidly changing environment dictates to the parties to take a short-run perspective of labour relations (Campbell, 1999). For various reasons, however, expired agreements continue to be in force with the understanding among the parties (Frenkel and Peetz, 1998). In a situation where capacity in trade unions in very limited, this arrangement cannot but put the latter at a disadvantage. Of equal importance is that there has been, in several countries, a declining trend in the use of collective bargaining itself, to a large extent due to the reluctance of some employers (or new investors) to use this machinery, and also to structural weaknesses and low capacity in trade unions.

Another associated effect, which the decentralisation of bargaining has only intensified in a number countries is the growing use of a new approach to workplace relations. Traditional industrial relations based on conflict and power relations are increasingly being called into question in the workplace (Fashoyin, 1998). The evolving management methods, particularly the human resource management approach seeks to give the enterprise a much enhanced role in workplace relations. In this era of global competition, a larger role for enterprise level relations is being emphasised. In such an approach, workers commitment and organisational integration are emphasised. Additionally, workplace flexibility, innovation and efficiency are today gaining more significance in labour–management relations.

3.2. Dispute Resolution and Role of the State

The introduction of democratic rule unleashed an unprecedented wave of (wild-cat) strikes in the affected countries as legal controls were relaxed or removed (Frenkel and Peetz, 1998; Fashoyin, 1998). Prevailing internal dispute resolution machinery had been less than clear, or in some cases, had been totally under the control of the employers. Public policy was in most cases less than decisive or fair to labour. Publicly administered machinery for dispute resolution was dominated by the state usually through the conciliation and mediation services of the Ministry of Labour. In cases such as this, the government exercised more than an administrative role; in many instances determining binding awards. However, the new democratic dispensation appears to have had a major effect on this area. Thus, as part of the labour law reform in the developing countries, the role of the state in dispute resolution has been changing to that of setting the framework for industrial relations and dispute resolution, and allowing the two sides of industry an enhanced role in resolving disputes. Public policy has also supported the evolution of independent third party mechanisms for dispute resolution.

Indeed, an important element of collective bargaining and sound industrial relations practice is the availability of an effective dispute resolution mechanism for dealing with the inevitable disagreement between workers and their employers in a fair and equitable manner. Today, equally important considerations, particularly in the developing countries, include the extent to which such mechanisms are available, and how participatory they are. However, while the severe impact of globalisation and economic reforms has somehow reduced the scope to which labour law reform on the free exercise of rights at work has been difficult to implement in a large number of countries, prevailing democratic dispensation in several developing countries has continued to induce governments to introduce fairly liberal regulation of the dispute resolution mechanisms.

The emerging laws, though quite different from one country to another, tend to allow a certain degree of the exercise of workers' right in employment relations. As part of the evolving systems, workers have several options to seek redress for their grievances. Third party intervention has become a major feature of dispute resolution in the era of globalisation. Arbitration and labour courts, often with a role for the social partners, have been established to resolve disputes which might not have been settled by the parties or through mediation. In quite a number of cases, independent and non-governmental conciliation and arbitration to resolve labour disputes. This trend to enhance the role of the partners in handling disputes with minimal state intervention is an important feature of emerging public policy in several developing countries. No doubt this direction of policy has the potential of strengthening labour-management relations and consolidating overall democracy.

4. EMERGING TRENDS AND CHALLENGES

4.1. *Changing Perception and Role of the Actors*

This world-wide concern about how the environment of work is organised and functions undoubtedly poses important challenges and opportunities for industrial relations actors. Clearly, the labour law reform and changing labour market are redefining both the institutions and processes of industrial relations. The role of the social partners, and that of the state are changing, just as their status and strategies on industrial relations. Importantly, despite the forcefulness of globalisation, it appears that governments have recognised the critical role of industrial relations in helping to address issues such as competitiveness on the one hand, and the promotion of workers rights on the other. In support of the inevitable consequences of globalisation and the new economic changes, labour legislation and institutions are increasingly featuring in public policy, in response to achieving a reasonable balance between economic efficiency and social protection for workers.

As a result of changing work environment and in particular the push for flexible employment policies, the social dimension of globalisation has been a subject of intense debate. It is increasingly recognised by governments, employers and workers' organisations that in order to consolidate the democracy, promote economic development in an atmosphere of peace, social equity, a minimum set of labour standards is important. With the acknowledgement that globalisation and other economic reforms policies have had adverse effects on the world of work, governments and employers are under international pressure to develop industrial relations policies in which the fundamental rights of the worker are respected, and that fair and equitable employment policies and rules prevail. These ideals as embodied in the ILO's Declaration of fundamental principles and rights at work are gaining acceptance in the developing countries (ILO, 2000). In the present decade, intensified efforts appear to be continuing at all fronts to ensure that industrial relations policies and practices fully reflect this view of the world of work. More importantly, industrial relations policies and practices will continue to attract attention as to the extent of their conformity to the fundamental principles and rights at work.

4.2. Tripartite Cooperation and Social Dialogue

The collapse of authoritarian regimes in Africa, Asia and Latin America have made unilateral control in the labour market an unrealistic practice. As a result the orientation of public policy is to create a totally different atmosphere which emphasises labour and management cooperation. While it might be tempting to overemphasise the extent of joint cooperation, there is no doubt that the commitment to address the challenges of globalisation and new economic realities are inducing greater cooperation among the stakeholders. Whether this inevitability can at this point be described as leading to a sustained cooperation is a matter of conjecture, but the trend appears to be emerging in which a win-win situation is the ultimate objective of the partners in the workplace. This pursuit of cooperation, at whatever scale or manner can be deciphered in at least two levels.

The first is at the enterprise level where in several developing countries, collective bargaining appears to have greater meaning and possibility. At the same time, it is the case that with the exception of a few countries, the practice of collective bargaining is minimal and indeed rudimentary in certain cases. Among the countries that use the machinery, marked differences exist as regards the extent, scope and use of collective bargaining for regulating employment conditions in the workplace. There are a few outstanding cases in the developing world where collective bargaining has attained high acceptability despite institutional or external impediments. In most cases, nonetheless, the thrust of collective bargaining and workplace relations is to create an environment in which joint approaches are used to solve industrial problems.

The second, related to bipartite relations between trade unions and employers, is higher-level consultation and cooperation. In most developing countries, for a multitude of reasons, including weak trade unions, unfavourable public policies, the role of tripartite cooperation for consensus building, particularly with regard to the formulation and implementation of economic and social policy have not been pursued. However, there is increasing recognition, particularly in government circles, that in order to effectively address the challenge of globalisation and the new economic realities it is no longer the case that government must retain exclusive authority over policy formulation. In most countries, tripartite institutions are being revitalised while new ones are being created to facilitate and strengthen concerted effort for reaching consensus on social and economic policies that affect the countries. This trend towards a concerted effort of government and the social partners in using social dialogue for achieving national consensus is transforming the respective roles of the industrial relations actors in the developing countries today.

Some illustrative cases stand out for mention. The Asian crisis which began in 1997 has had the positive effect of creating the awareness of the critical role of social dialogue as a veritable mechanism through which the economic turmoil could be addressed. In the aftermath of the crisis, tripartite consultation, intended to bring about a concerted solution to the economic problem, was spear-headed in several countries. In Thailand and Philippines, it was the crisis that induced a renewed interest in the tripartite approach to problem-solving. In the particular case of Malaysia, the initiative to use this mechanism was taken by the top political leadership (Campbell, 1999). The experience of African and Latin America are practically the same, as developing countries are realising the valuable role of joint effort in addressing major economic and social problems (Bronstein, 1995, Fashoyin, 1998). In South Africa and Malawi, for example, political realities and the concern for rapid economic development induced a resort to broad participatory machinery to address economic and labour market problems.

These efforts are significant developments because, quite distinct from the traditional approach to tripartite consultation on labour market issues, the resort to social dialogue in East Asia and several other developing countries has been based on the conviction that it was a suitable mechanism for popular participation in solving macro economic problems. In countries such as Barbados, tripartite institutions and processes which were created solely to deal with prevailing economic problems have been retained as permanent mechanisms for social dialogue. There is hardly any doubt that tripartite cooperation, or efforts to bring the major stakeholders to socio-economic policy formulation and implementation, will continue to be a key feature of industrial relations in the developing countries in the future.

BIBLIOGRAPHY

Arturo S. Bronstein, 'Societal change and industrial relations in Latin America: Trends and prospects'. *International Labour Review*, Vol. 143, No. 2, 1995.

Duncan Campbell, 'Globalization and Change: Social dialogue and labour market adjustment in the crisis-affected countries of East Asia'. Bangkok, ILO/EASMAT, 1999.

Maria L. Cook, 'Toward flexible industrial relations? Neo-liberalism, democracy, and labour reform in Latin America'. *Industrial Relations*, Vol. 37, No. 3 July 1998.

Tayo Fashoyin, *Industrial relations in southern Africa: The challenge of change*. Harare, ILO/SAMAT, Policy Paper No. 5, 1998.

Stephen J. Frenkel and David Peetz, 'Globalization and industrial relations in East Asia: A three-country comparison', *Industrial Relations*, Vol. 37, No. 3, July 1998.

ILO, *Collective bargaining: A fundamental principle, a right, a convention*. Geneva, Labour Education, 1999.

ILO, *Industrial relations, democracy and social stability*. Geneva, World Labour Report, 1997.

ILO, *Your voice at work*. Geneva, General Report on the Declaration, 2000

IMF, *Globalization, opportunities and challenges*. Washington, DC, World Economic Outlook, May 1997.

C.S. Venkata Ratnam and D.P.A. Naidu, *Industrial relations and collective bargaining in South Asia*. New Delhi, ILO/SAAT, 1999,

Richard Sandbrook, 'Democratization and the implementation of economic reform in Africa' *Journal of International Development*, Vol. 8, No. 1, 1996.

Henk Thomas, *Globalization and Third World trade unions*. London, Zed Press, 1995.

NOTE

[1]   This is a revised version of a presentation to the students from the Institute for Labour Relations, University of Leuven, Belgium first in 1997 and then in 2000.

Peter Auer

4. EMPLOYMENT REVIVAL IN EUROPE[1]

Small countries on the way to success

1. INTRODUCTION

During the last twenty years the conventional wisdom has been that the European labour market is "sclerotic", in stark contrast to the dynamic US labour market. The USA has experienced much higher growth rates of employment and markedly lower unemployment than Europe. Despite GDP growth rates which were comparable with the US over the long term and at times even higher, economic growth contributed only very marginally to an expansion of employment. Unemployment also continued to grow in the European Union, reaching around 11% of the labour force in the middle of the nineties, and has only very recently started to fall below the 10% threshold.

The causes of US success were widely seen in its free market approach, flexible wages resulting in high income differentiation and low employment protection resulting in flexibly adjusting employment. The prescription of leading economists for Europe was to use the same ingredients as those which were believed to be at the core of American success. Deregulation and privatisation were to lead to a retreat of governments and the social partners from intervention in the markets. An entrepreneurial spirit, relieved from the straitjacket of rules and regulations, and a wage policy left to the needs of the market would finally result in an improvement of the economy and the labour market and (re)establish the positive dynamics of the market forces everywhere.

Core elements of the European model, such as corporatist and often centralised collective bargaining leading to high and downwardly rigid wages, ever expanding social and employment protection and the strong role of the state in the sociol-economy, were seen as the culprits in Europe's labour market problems. Unemployment was declared to be structural and voluntary, in the sense that rational actors on the labour markets would not take up work, if there were alternatives of "making unemployment pay" in the form of overgenerous benefits. In addition, high levels of public involvement and employment were denounced as displacing private

R. Blanpain and C. Engels (eds), The ILO and the Social Challenge of the 21st Century, 45–59.
© 2001 *Kluwer Law International. Printed in Great Britain.*

initiatives, for example in the service sector. Clearly, in such an approach there was no place for government to regulate the economy. Aggregate demand was seen as the outcome of the interplay of the market forces and if supply was flexible enough "it would create its own demand", as J.B. Say had postulated back in the early 19th century. And according to the concept of the natural rate of unemployment (M. Friedman, 1968) government intervention would only result in higher inflation. In a nutshell the visible hand of government and the social partners should give way to the invisible hand of market forces.

While there was opposition in many European countries to the adoption of these supply side policies, observers agree that during the last decade supply side considerations have dominated the debate and have also been policy driving in Europe. A reminder of the major recent policy debates in Europe shows this quite strikingly: In the forefront of the debate and policy making stood neither fiscal expansion, regulation, extension of public employment and nationalisation nor the expansion of the social security network, but rather supply side reforms, deregulation, privatisation and the curbing of public jobs. Countries like France which in the early eighties put the policies of the "old" demand side agenda into practice for a brief period, followed many of the prescriptions of the "new" supply side agenda after 1982.

Today a number of smaller European countries have seen such a major fall in unemployment that one can speak of labour market recovery and relative success at last. Consequently, one of the questions of the present study is whether the application of the above policies has contributed to the success of the four countries under review. To be frank from the outset: we do not believe that recent labour market success can be categorically explained by the retreat of the government and the social partners, by deregulation, privatisation, reduced public jobs or lean organisation. Although such policies might have made a contribution to labour market success, the main explanation lies elsewhere: it is not the countries which have reduced social spending most, have curbed government intervention drastically or minimised social partnership which are today leading success cases. It is rather those which have retained, while adapting, their institutions, which today see their economic success spilling over onto the labour market. It is therefore not the flexibility of the market, but the existence and adaptability of institutions and regulations, which explains success in the cases reviewed. Contrary to widespread assumptions, they were not in fact too rigid to survive in an environment demanding greater adaptability. The special European way of dealing with change, filtering it through its established labour market institutions, leads to positive results. In other words, in Europe the "baby was not thrown out with the bath water". The baby (institutions) was kept and the water (inefficiencies in the institutions) was at least partially thrown out and this accounts for a large part of European success.

2. RELATIVE LABOUR MARKET SUCCESS

While the European Union as a total still has high unemployment rates which have only recently fallen below the 10 percent mark, some of the smaller European countries have in fact a much better labour market record. For the sake of this study four smaller European countries were chosen because of a variety of reasons: they all are experiencing recently a fall in unemployment and some of them have managed to have employment growth rates similar to those of the US job machine. But besides such criteria, there have also been other considerations, such as the consent of the governing body of the ILO and the willingness of countries to participate in the studies.

Chart 1 in the annex and Table 1 below show that the four countries under review have succeeded in curbing unemployment. In addition some of the countries have recently seen a rapid increase in employment and in the employment intensity of economic growth, which shows that fears of jobless growth are – at least for the employment generating service sector- unfounded. (see Table 2). Also employment rates (the share of the employed in the population of working age) have increased in all four countries. The differences between male and female employment rates have generally been reduced, but remain large, especially if employment rates in full-time equivalents are considered, because of many women working part-time. Youth unemployment has also continued to decline, as did long-term unemployment.

This success is particularly visible, when the four countries are compared to some of the bigger countries in Europe,[2] which still suffer from depressed labour markets with sometimes very high levels of unemployment, youth and long-term unemployment. While unemployment in Ireland has declined rapidly, it is still high compared with the three other countries. However, it has now fallen significantly below the EU average. Ireland is also experiencing a fast decline in youth and long-term unemployment, however from a high level.

Austria, which has maintained low levels of unemployment over a long period, had lately seen a small increase, but has most recently succeeded in a decrease. In addition it has both low youth and long-term unemployment.

Even if Dutch unemployment levels are now below the threshold of the traditional definition of full employment (3%), none of the countries has yet reached full employment if qualitative criteria are also included. In addition, the official unemployment rate, based on the ILO definition[3] does not show the real extent of joblessness, as some unemployment is hidden.[4] There is some way to go before we can speak of absolute and not relative success. However, while this employment success has been accompanied by a change in the structure of employment from permanent full-time jobs to a more heterogeneous pattern of jobs (such as part-time and temporary jobs), it seems that the labour markets have not (yet) changed dramatically. In fact, permanent full-time and part-time jobs are still the dominant form of employment in European labour markets and flexible jobs rather marginal (at least measured in stock terms). Also job tenure is only slightly declining and it seems that declining tenure for men is to a certain extent offset by rising tenure of women. An ILO study (Auer,Cazes, forthcoming) will deal in detail with this question.

The overall conclusion concerning rising wage inequalities, which are often seen as a corollary to rising employment, is that at least three of the countries, which belong

47

Peter Auer

Table 1. Unemployment change February 1998/February 2000, seasonally adjusted (%)

	Total			Male			Female			Gender gap**	
	February 1998	February 2000	Change (%)	February 1998	February 2000	Change (%)	February 1998	February 2000	Change (%)	Change (%)	February 2000
Austria	4.6	3.5	−23%	3.9	3.1	−20%	5.6	4.2	−25%	−25%	1.1
Denmark	5.3	4.9	−7%	4.1	4.2	+2%	6.8	5.6	−18%	−18%	1.4
Ireland	8.4	5.1	−40%	8.6	5.1	−41%	8.1	5.1	−37%	−37%	0.0
Netherlands	4.6	2.7*	−41%	3.5	2.1*	−40%	6.1*	3.6	−41%	−41%	1.5
EU	10.2	8.8	−13%	8.8	7.5	−15%	12.1	10.4	−14%	−14%	1.6

Source: Eurostat press release March 2000. Internet version.
* January 2000.
**Difference male : female unemployment rate.

Table 2. GDP growth and employment growth 1985–1998 and 1994–1997/annual average growth rates

	GDP		Employment		Employment intensity*	
	(1)	(2)	(1)	(2)	(1)	(2)
Austria	2.50	2.10	0.56	0.20	0.224	0.00
Denmark	2.04	2.70	0.46	1.70	0.225	0.70
Ireland	5.84	9.90	1.26	4.40	0.215	0.62
Netherlands	2.80	3.00	1.87	2.20	0.668	0.73
EU 15	2.13	1.70	0.44	0.50	0.207	0.20
USA	2.55	3.30	1.47	1.90	0.576	0.60

*Employment/GDP = percentage points of employment created for 1% of economic growth (1) 1985–1998, (2) 1994–1997.
Source: ILO CEPR comparative report on the basis of OECD, Employment Outlook 1998, figures for 1998 are estimates; European Commission, Employment in Europe 1998.

to the Northern and Central European socio-economic model, produce less inequalities than those which are based on a free market approach.[5] In fact, the countries analysed here, show a better efficiency/equity balance as for example the USA.

3. SOCIAL DIALOGUE

This results from collective bargaining between the social partners within systems of "corporatist governance"[6] but is also due to the efficiency of the social transfer system in poverty reduction which itself can be considered as an outcome of the social dialogue. While the social transfer system has been much criticised for inefficiently allocating public money, such criticism has certainly been blunted by the recent changes introduced in the system, especially the "activating" elements in labour market policies. This will make it increasingly more difficult to draw "passive" unemployment benefits (e.g. those not traded off for participation in intensive job search training or job creation schemes) for long periods.

Historically, an insufficiently developed social dialogue had contributed to the employment crisis in the seventies and early eighties, triggered by the two oil crisis. At that time the social dialogue experienced problems and the approach was often more adversarial and ideologically charged. However, when the social dialogue became more pragmatic and oriented towards problem solving, it contributed importantly to employment success. A new concerted effort by social partners and governments to tackle the pending problems that had afflicted Europe in the 1980s and early 1990s, as weak competitiveness and a worsening employment situation, has finally permitted some countries to emerge from crisis.

In three of the countries under review, such a concerted effort is witnessed by the conclusion of social pacts of a national dimension: the first was concluded in 1982 in the Netherlands (the Wassenaar Agreement), followed by the "Declaration of Intent" in Denmark and the "Programme for National Recovery" in Ireland, both signed in

1987. The pacts expressed the desire of the partners to cooperate in order to solve the problems facing the economy through a concerted approach based on wage moderation and a boost in competitiveness, while maintaining but reforming the welfare state. Typical trade-offs for moderate wage increases were tax cuts, working time reductions and labour market policy measures (e.g. measures to cushion employment adjustment). Concerted action between the social partners and the government has been the traditional way of governance in Austria, and no new pact has been concluded. However, there, too, the system was confronted with new challenges, such as the privatisation of the nationalised industries or the reform of social security.

While in other countries, such as the UK and New Zealand, the crisis ended in the dismantling of much of the existing social dialogue and its institutions, in the countries under review, the song of the "sirens of deregulation" (Alan, 1997) actually had the effect of reinvigorating the social dialogue. The governments in these countries usually took a leading role in bringing the partners together to the bargaining table, designing and/or endorsing reform plans and in financing parts of the trade-offs for wage moderation. The state was therefore a very proactive agent of change.

4. MACROECONOMIC POLICY

Not only the social dialogue and the reforms it has made possible, also the macroeconomic environment and macroeconomic policy have been important factors to explain the success of these countries. The macroeconomic environment in Europe in general is today much healthier than in the seventies and eighties: low inflation, low interest rates, moderate wage growth and consolidated government budgets have restored confidence in the economies. It seems to be accepted that fairly tight monetary policies have helped to create this environment, as has moderate wage growth as an essential result of the social dialogue. Economic growth has been driven by foreign and domestic demand, the share of the former tending to increase over the nineties, but the latter seems to have staged a temporary comeback as foreign demand weakened in the wake of the Asian crisis. Also domestic and foreign investments have boosted growth and employment. Last but not least, government consumption are also part of this favourable situation. Despite claims that government expenses tend to crowd out private demand and investments, it rather seems that the expenditure elements of GDP are mutually supportive (Schettkat, forthcoming). While structural elements of the budget have become more important, in some countries (e.g. Denmark) government expenditure has been used in a targeted and short-term manner and has supported upswings without creating inflationary pressures. At least two of the countries experienced a de facto devaluation (by moderate wage policies) against some of their major (European) trade partners and this has also spurred their economies (Hartog, 1999). However, claims that "beggar-thy-neighbour" policies are the major factors behind superior economic performance, seem exaggerated.

Tax policies have been changed, resulting lately in a reduction of social contributions for the low wage sector and (in some countries) a decrease in the highest rates in the tax progression. Corporate taxes have also been lowered and might have stimulated investments.[7] Tax revenues have risen in absolute figures but declined as a share of GDP in Ireland and the Netherlands. But in Denmark and Austria, increased revenue has also been used to create additional public jobs and has not hindered Denmark in triggering off a general improvement of its economy and the labour market. However, there are still many differences in tax structures and they might distort competition in Europe. The realisation of the EMU will in future increase pressure for a harmonisation not only of monetary, fiscal and wage policies, but also of tax policies.

5. LABOUR MARKET POLICY

Both active and passive labour market policy are important policy tools to regulate employment and unemployment. The study has found some evidence that unemployment benefit systems and other passive labour market policy instruments such as early retirements are not only mechanisms to protect workers but allow also flexible employment adjustment for companies. Especially unemployment systems, which are used de jure or de facto as lay-off systems provide an important flexibility buffer, in particular for smaller firms. The percentage of those unemployed returning to their employer after a short duration unemployment spell shows this convincingly.

Early retirement has provided exit flexibility for firms and allowed workers to enjoy a better status than being unemployed at the end of their working lives. Invalidity pension systems have also been used for labour market purposes. While this supply reduction policies explain some of the successes of the past, the continuation of these policies might pose a challenge for the future. The ageing of the workforce and the high costs of the "easy exit" solution, which can also go together with a loss of experienced "human capital", require new solutions. Cuts in the systems, with the aim of reducing costs, might lead to an increase in unemployment for older workers. Therefore, such necessary cuts should be implemented carefully and preferably if other alternatives (namely new jobs for older workers) exist, or if firms are willing to maintain employment relationships with their older workforce. In any case income security at the end of working life, before regular retirement is an important element of the European system of social protection.

Many smaller (administrative) reforms have been undertaken in the unemployment protection systems in almost all of the countries under review, some of which have also produced the intended effect. In Denmark, for example, restriction on the access of poorly educated youth to benefits by linking benefit payment to an obligatory participation in education had a tangible effect on youth unemployment. However, this is much more a policy of activation (as it compensates restrictions on the passive side with offers on the active side) and the study found that in general policies of activation are more promising than administrative changes alone.

In all countries, but to very different degrees, active labour market policy, a second best solution after regular employment, have played an important role in the recovery.

51

Especially in Denmark such measures have been used quite substantially. There are however considerable differences between countries as to the distribution between active and passive policies. As evaluation research has shown, the impact of active labour market policy might also be reduced through deadweight or substitution effects. However, the weight of active labour market measures is bound to increase because of the effects of the European Employment Strategy with its goal to increase employment, employability and the employment rate.

In addition, as the employment systems are bound to change towards more flexibility, a large number of people will transit between jobs, between jobs and unemployment, between jobs and training, and between jobs and (parental) leave schemes etc. These transitions will also need to be accompanied by labour market policies, ensuring a bridge between work and non-work (Schmid, G., 1995; Gazier, G., 1999).

6. COUNTRY-SPECIFIC FACTORS

While the three policies (macroeconomic, social dialogue and labour market policies) in their specific combination explain a large part of the success of the countries in their labour markets, there are also specific reasons in each of the countries. For example, Ireland has attracted a large part of foreign direct investment in a strategic growth sector – information technology – which has resulted in high growth rates. European structural funds money has also contributed to GDP growth. The Netherlands have been world champions in the creation of part-time jobs, often in conjunction with an increase in the activities of temporary work agencies. Austria has benefited from the opening of the Eastern markets and Denmark has enacted a policy of job rotation and training leaves fitting well with its other institutional features such as a lay-off system and comprehensive adult training. All countries have also developed specific clusters of production (e.g. transport in the Netherlands, IT in Ireland, car parts in Austria) which have been growth intensive.

7. COMBINATION EFFECTS

More than from isolated policy actions, labour market success seems to result from an efficient combination of factors. Our study offers some indications on how such interactions might work. At the macroeconomic level, tight monetary policy, fiscal consolidation and wage moderation policies seem to have accommodated each other and the Austria is a good example of how to introduce long term stability by such a coordination of policies.

More specifically, on the labour markets in Denmark and Austria, weak dismissal protection (on the regulation side in Denmark and "de-facto" in Austria) seems to go together with relatively strong (income) protection at the societal level (whereby unemployment benefits are higher in Denmark than in Austria). In these countries, where small and medium-sized firms prevail, such systems seem to support the economy and the labour market and add to flexibility, resulting in low shares of long-term unemployment. These countries have also high employment rates. For small firms and the seasonal sector and its workforce, this arrangement seems to be a stabilising factor, although it involves some cross-subsidisation. As can be seen by the case of Austria, this does not preclude the extension of flexible working time to cope with some of the strong seasonal fluctuation.

Other such efficient combinations include the temporary demand injection in the economy combined with a training-based job rotation scheme in Denmark; or the combination of part-time work, a basic pension scheme and placement activities of temporary work agencies in the Netherlands.

In general, systemic elements working in the same direction are more efficient than elements working in opposite directions. If systemic elements in employment systems are congruent, employment performance is better. The Danish employment system might be taken as an example of how such elements interact: high labour turnover is supported not only by the lay-off system, but also by labour market training, which itself is congruent with training leave schemes. Denmark also has both parental leave schemes and child care provisions which result in more possibilities for women to participate in working life.

Combination of policies, which result in both flexibility for firms and security for workers might be the most appropriate institutional arrangements in European labour markets. To varying degrees at least three of the four countries have managed to have such arrangements.

However, given the complexity of these systems thorough research is needed to determine the precise effect of such combinations. Timing is also important: temporary leave schemes might be efficient bridges to the regular labour market in the upswing, but possibly not in a downturn, as most of the leavers will probably once again be unemployed after their leave. In an unpredictable and complex world, such combinations and the right timing also need some luck in order to add up to successful policies.

8. DO SMALL COUNTRIES HAVE SPECIFIC ADVANTAGES?

The countries under review are small, only the Netherlands can be considered middle sized. The four countries account for around 10% of European Union GDP and around 9% of its total labour force.

While the three factors of a sound macroeconomic environment and policy, the

Table 3. GDP and labour force (LF) in percent of total EU, 1996

Austria		Denmark		Ireland		Netherlands	
GDP	LF	GDP	LF	GDP	LF	GDP	LF
2.44	2.28	2.00	1.67	0.90	0.88	4.43	4.44

Source: ILO CEPR data bank.

53

social dialogue and labour market policy might produce their effects also in bigger countries, the mere smallness of the countries under review might be an additional factor of success. Katzenstein (1985) has outlined some of the factors, which distinguish small from larger industrialised countries: the first of such factors is the economic openness, which is in part due to the small size of domestic markets. "Dependence on imports and the necessity to export make the economies of the small European states both more open and more specialised than those of larger countries" (Katzenstein, 1985, p. 87). Secondly, democratic corporatism based on an ideology of social partnership, a system of centralised and concentrated interest groups and voluntary and informal coordination of conflicting objectives. However, while there might be some other advantage in being small, such as a more homogeneous labour force and better governability (and thus better cooperation between actors), this alone cannot be an important factor as most of the countries went through a major crisis before their present recovery. It could be however, that once a successful system of "corporatist governance" is established or reinvigorated, smallness becomes again a distinct advantage, because of the smaller "power elite" circles. This in turn leads to more informality and closer personal relationships which is an important condition for successful bargaining and consensus. This is certainly one of the reasons for the success of the Austrian system of social partnership. The system was run in the seventies by powerful leaders on both sides, which have since given way to a somewhat more depersonalised style of governance. Not least because of the danger of such systems becoming top heavy, there must be a continuous connection with their constituents, in order to ensure adequate interest representation. The skill of governance in corporatist governance systems is to represent group interests and match them with the interests of the larger economy. This is not always easy. For example, the latest bargaining round in Denmark was ended by government intervention because the union bargainers were not followed by their rank and file.

9. WHAT CAN OTHER COUNTRIES LEARN FROM SMALL COUNTRIES?

It is not only smallness which is important here, but the traditions and cultures which are the background of different institutions, and which might make it more difficult to understand and transfer experience from one country to the other. In particular, it might be very difficult to adapt "democratic corporatism" in countries with a liberal, pluralist tradition of policy formulation.

However, smaller countries can teach at least two lessons to bigger European countries. Firstly while "democratic corporatism" per se is not the answer to all labour market problems, it seems that once a real dialogue is established within the overall framework of corporatism, solutions to the problems can be found. This also shows that problems are never purely economical but have always a political dimension, which relates to the forms of governance. And corporatism seems to be a form of governance which is of equal efficiency in running the economy as liberal pluralist (market-led) forms of governance. Especially if equity issues are taken into account, corporatist governance has clearly superior performance. The problem of corporatist governance countries was up to now their failing employment performance. With this problem solved, the countries seem to have developed into successful socio-economic models. And although the bigger countries like France, Germany, Italy and Spain have also their form of social dialogue, they have experienced many problems in the recent past. We can remind here of the difficulties to set up a social concertation (Bündnis für Arbeit) in Germany – which by the way is at the present more successful and has very recently helped to trigger reforms and a better economic climate in Germany, which can be seen as a proof of the fact that the social dialogue helps to carry through necessary reforms. Also France has experienced many problems in its dialogue (this is due also to the divisions within the labour movement) but the 35 hours law has certainly renewed at least company bargaining and the state has often acted as "functional equivalent" to what in other countries has been done by the social partners. But both countries have not yet solved their unemployment problem and should use the dialogue to do so.

The second lesson is that economic openness pays off and that there seem to be no longer-term negative effects of globalisation on the labour markets of industrialised countries, or at least no such problems which remain unsolved. Besides these two major elements (form of governance and degree of economic openness) there are many other examples of policy elements from the four success cases, which might help some of the bigger European countries to overcome their labour market problems. For example, there is no reason why bigger countries should not be able to introduce job rotation schemes along the Danish lines or part-time regulations like the Dutch. A job rotation system (adapted from the Danish model) was, for example, recently introduced in Austria, which has rather similar institutions to Germany. Especially concerning part-time work, equal treatment with full-time work is important. There could also be advantages in having a three-pillar financing system for retirement (a basic pension, a contribution based system and a private top-up) like in Denmark or in the Netherlands, in other countries as well. And the Austrian (and German) apprenticeship system may well still serve as a model for the introduction of alternative training in other countries. These are only some examples out of many which show that it is not impossible to transfer elements of one system to another. It is almost certain that such convergence of policies and regulations will be stimulated by the European Monetary Union, which will inevitably lead to more adjustment in various policy fields.

Another of these "convergence drivers" is the European Employment Strategy. The common guidelines and the associated monitoring process must be expected to lead to more convergence in employment and labour market policies.

We will refrain from a discussion of the transferability of elements of the small European cases to countries outside the realm of the core industrialised countries. This problem cannot be addressed without a thorough analysis of the institutional and economic conditions in these other countries (e.g. the transition countries or the developing countries). Concerning the form of governance, "democratic corporatism" could serve as a model for governance, but the political prerequisites (e.g. strong and equal partners) are usually not met. However, even grass-root corporatism at local level could be later on developed in a more centralised form of democratic corporatism. In any case, there seems to be no real alternative to a dialogue between social actors in order to have some governability in the economy and this basic principle could apply world-wide.

However, concerning the form of governance, "democratic corporatism" could serve as a model for governance, if the political prerequisites (e.g. strong and equal partners, an openness and a will to discuss problems and to let the social partners participate in decision making, as well as institutions of the dialogue) are at least partially met. And even grass-root corporatism at local level could be later on developed in a more encompassing form of democratic corporatism. In any case, there seems to be no real alternative to a dialogue between social actors in order to have some governability in the economy and this basic principle could apply world-wide.

Another lesson is that you need both a good mix of passive and active labour market policies in order to have both a functioning and sustainable economy and labour market. This can be seen for example in Asia. Up to the recent crisis existing active labour market policies were usually designed to cope with labour shortages and human resource development (Inagami, 1998). During the crisis, however, the lack of other adjustment policies, and in particular an unemployment insurance, had an impact both on poverty and the maintenance of the employability of the workers. Lee (1999), noticing the lack of an unemployment insurance, puts forward some of the reasons why such protection systems have not been installed. Among these reasons were the uninterrupted path of development up to the crisis with only short term problems and a belief in the absorption capacities of the informal sector (and the families) as a safety net. He advances also that the adepts of the so called "Asian values" rejected the assistance image linked to the generous western welfare system. In addition the idea of the employment destroying effects of high non-wage labour costs going together with contribution based unemployment benefit systems, might also have acted as a barrier.

One could add, that the interpretation of an unemployment system as a device whose only function is to protect workers might also have contributed to the "institutional passivity" of these governments. In fact, and our study shows this clearly, unemployment systems and active labour market policies have two functions not only in a time of crisis: they allow for basic income and social protection, but also for adjustment flexibility of companies. They are effective buffers around firms and relieve them from some of their social responsibility (which many of the larger and smaller "paternalistically" governed firms in fact have) in socialising some of the risks of economic life. This is certainly one of the lessons of the four country study which could be of relevance for the developing world in general.

10. CONCLUSION

In conclusion the relative labour market success of the four countries is due partly to country-specific factors and partly to the social dialogue, macroeconomic policy and labour market policy and specific combination of these and other policies. The social dialogue achieved a climate of confidence among the major social actors. Wage moderation contributed to the new climate of confidence and considerable reforms in the social protection systems were enacted, mostly within a climate of negotiation and consensus.

Wage moderation was also the corollary of a stabilisation oriented macroeconomic policy which led to low inflation and low interest rates. Labour market policy (and social protection in general) created the necessary flexibility for adjustment on the labour markets. Labour market policies and social protection schemes should therefore not only be seen as a device to secure income to those without work, but also a sort of "buffer" zone around regular labour markets enabling firms to shed labour without paying all the economic and social costs. Early retirement schemes, which have contributed to success are, with lay-off and training systems such as in Denmark, good examples for this. However, in face of workforce ageing, first signs of labour shortages and high costs the social protection system has recently been reformed in all of the countries. Early retirement possibilities have been restricted and labour market policy activated.

This might only mean that the welfare state – which we see part and parcel of the success of these countries in achieving an efficiency/equity balance-shifts from a society which distributes wealth partly through social transfers to a society which aims at the participation of a maximum of people in primary revenue resulting from work. However, there must also be a role of passive labour market policies in the future, precisely because of its buffer role. Such an "embedded" labour market, for which the right portion of active and passive labour market policies are used, is an alternative to a labour market subject overwhelmingly to the law of supply and demand in which workers would shoulder the brunt of adjustment hardship.

In any case, while the four countries differ in many respects and have by no means achieved "the best of all worlds" they have made progress towards the goal of full employment. Much remains to be done, but these countries have shown that employment success is also feasible in Europe's welfare states that maintain a balance between economic and social issues.

BIBLIOGRAPHY

Auer, P. (2000): *Employment Revival in Europe: Labour Market Success in Austria, Denmark, Ireland and the Netherlands*, ILO, Geneva.

Auer, P., Cazes, S.: *Job stability and flexibility in OECD countries* (working title), ILO, forthcoming.

Bertola,G .; Boeri, T.; Cazes, S. (2000): *Labour Market Regulations in Industrialized Countries.* "The case for new indicators" in: International Labour Review, Volume 139, Number 1, p. 57–72, ILO, Geneva.

Bosch, G., *From the Redistribution to the Modernisation of Working Time*, ILO forthcoming.

Frühstück, E., Gregoritsch, P., Löffler, R., Wagner-Pinter, M. (1998): *Die Rückkehr in ein vorübergehend aufgelöstes Beschäftigungsverhältnis*, Synthesis, AMS, Wien.

Gazier, B. (1999): *What are Transitional Labour markets?*, Paper prepared for the Translam Conference in Berlin.

Hartog, J. (1999): *The Netherlands: So, What's so special about the Dutch model?*, Employment and Training Paper No. 54, ILO, Geneva.

Inagami, T. (1998): *Labour market policies in Asian countries: Diversity and similarity among Singapore, Malaysia, the Republic of Korea and Japan*, Employment and Training Paper No. 34, ILO, Geneva.

Katzenstein, P.J. (1985): *Small States in World Markets, Industrial Policy in Europe*, Cornell University Press, Ithaca.

Lee, E. (1998): *The Asian financial crisis*, ILO, Geneva.

Madsen, P.K. (1999): *Denmark: Flexibility, security and labour market success*, Employment and Training Paper No. 53, ILO, Geneva.

O'Connell, Ph. (1999): *Astonishing success and the labour market in Ireland*, Employment and Training Paper No. 44, ILO, Geneva.

OECD, (1998, 1997): *Economic Surveys: Austria, Denmark, Ireland, the Netherlands*, Paris: OECD.

OECD, (1996): *Jobs Study, Implementing the Strategy*, Paris: OECD.

Pichelmann, K., Hofer, H.(1999): *Austria: Long-term success through social partnership*, Employment and Training Paper No. 52, ILO, Geneva.

Rubery, J.: *Equal Opportunites and Employment Policy*, ILO, forthcoming.

Schettkat, R.: *Small Economy Macroeconomics*, ILO, forthcoming.

Schmid, G. (1995), "Is full Employment still Possible? Transitional Labour Markets as a New Strategy of Labour Market Policy" in: *Economic and Industrial Policy*, 11 pp. 429–456.

Visser, J.: *Social Dialogue and Industrial Relations in Austria, Denmark, Ireland and the Netherlands*, ILO forthcoming.

NOTES

1   The present comparative study is part of the ILO's follow up activities to Commitment Three of the Declaration and Programme of Action of the World Summit on Social Development in Copenhagen in 1995. Commitment Three reiterates the importance of full, productive and freely chosen employment, as a basic condition for social progress. The study reviews labour market progress in Austria, Denmark, Ireland and the Netherlands as part of the overall framework of Country Employment Policy Reviews, which are also undertaken in other, less developed regions of the world. This paper is a summary of a recent ILO book: Peter Auer, Employment Revival in Europe: Labour Market Success in Austria, Denmark, Ireland and the Netherlands. ILO, Geneva, 2000. A slightly modified version of this paper will be presented at the 12th IIRA World Congress in Tokyo.

2   (Especially the four accounting for most of the high European unemployment rate: Italy, Germany, France and Spain, although they have also recently managed to reduce unemployment).

3   To be classified as unemployed, the respondent to the survey has to be without work, has to be available for work and has to actively have searched for work in the reference period.

4   For a discussion of the concept see page 25 ff. In Auer, P.,2000.

5   Although there seem to be considerable differences between the four countries (e.g. there is evidence that income inequalities have risen more in Ireland and also in the Netherlands than in Denmark and Austria. O'Connell, 1999; Hartog, 1999).

6   "Corporatist governance" or "democratic corporatism" is a system of governance, in which the three main social and economic actors (the government, employers and workers representatives) shape and even implement policies through the social dialogue, which manifests itself through national, regional and local pacts, traditional collective bargaining and the administration of parts of the employment and social protection schemes.

7   The lowest rates are found in Ireland, and the Irish government was also accused by its European partners to have attracted foreign direct investment because of this low rate.

11. ANNEX 1

Unemplyment rates (ILO-definition) 1980–1999

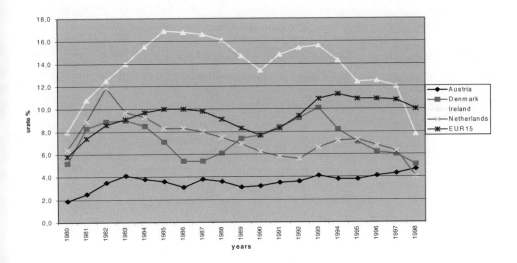

Deborah France

5. EMPLOYERS AND THE INTERNATIONAL LABOUR ORGANISATION

1. Introduction

Before I begin I would like to explain who I am and how I came to be involved in the employer world, particularly here in Geneva. I joined the IOE last year after ten years of representing the interests of British employers internationally. My main responsibilities were working on European social affairs issues, the social chapter and all that and I sat on a number of consultative committees in Brussels. At the same time, I was lucky enough to be elected a titular employer member of the ILO's Governing Body and became a member of its Committee on Freedom of Association. So my association with the ILO goes back over ten years now.

During my time with the British employers I was always amazed that international issues were given so little attention by both employer associations and their company members. Maybe they were operating on the premise that international organisations are too remote to be a threat, or that issues in the international world seem intangible and unreal and will never affect the day to day lives of companies and their employees, I don't know. That might have been true for some companies twenty years ago, but is certainly not true now.

The last five years have seen a sea change in the way in which international developments can have a domestic impact. Of course in Europe the international organisation which has the most domestic impact is the European Union and no business can afford to ignore developments there. Nevertheless, the impact of an organisation such as the ILO remains largely ignored by the wider business community. At a time when the ILO is in danger of becoming relevant, this is not a satisfactory state of affairs.

When I joined the IOE last year, one of my main tasks was to identify the potential impact the ILO has on business and to try to promote a greater awareness of the organisation. I have to say that progress has been slow. I will outline some of the main challenges we are facing for you later on but first of all it might be useful if I briefly outline the organisation I work for, its mission and its key activities.

R. Blanpain and C. Engels (eds), The ILO and the Social Challenge of the 21st Century, 61–63.
© 2001 *Kluwer Law International. Printed in Great Britain.*

2. The International Organisation of Employers

The IOE was founded in 1920 as an organisation that would provide the secretariat for the employers' group at the newly founded ILO. Its main tasks are the following:

- Defending employer interests at the international level, particularly within the ILO
- Promoting the development of free enterprise
- Strengthening national employers' organisations
- Facilitating the transfer of information and experience to employers' organisations.

Currently we have 127 national employers' organisations in membership world-wide. These include members from north and south, and developed and developing countries. The criteria for membership are fairly straightforward. To join, an organisation must be a national representative organisation of employers, represent free enterprise and be voluntary, independent and free from external influence. Our main policy making organ is our General Council that meets annually. The Management Board, which meets three times a year, is responsible for strategic policy and financial decisions. The General Secretariat is based in Geneva and assures the day to day activities of the organisation.

The main responsibility of the IOE has been related to the ILO. We provide the Secretariat for the various ILO meetings ranging from the Governing Body and its committees, the Annual International Labour Conference to the numerous sectoral and technical meetings that take place during the year. We are part advisers, part technicians and part lobbiests. We are also involved in numerous technical co-operation projects with our members on issues such as child labour, strengthening employer organisations and so on.

For many years the IOE saw the ILO as its key focus. The problem was that the fortunes of the IOE were tied up to the fortunes of the ILO. And this was a very real problem. For many European federations in particular, the ILO was seen as irrelevant, particularly as they grew more and more used to dealing with Brussels. It was seen as anti-business and far removed from the real world of work. Therefore if the ILO was irrelevant, why have an IOE? As the ILO sank into obscurity in the 70's and 80's, fewer employer associations were ready to give time and resource to the organisation. As the 90's approached the IOE was faced with a choice: should it reform itself or just reconcile itself to being a very small secretariat that serviced employer participants at ILO meetings?

If we had carried on in the way we were operating we perhaps would not exist now. But we were saved by a challenge and the challenge is that of globalisation which has had an impact on labour and social affairs and the ILO as it has had an impact on every other policy area of interest to business. This has enabled us to begin to explain to our members in clearer terms the potential role the ILO can play and the relevance it has to the business community. Globalisation has had a number of effects on the way the IOE acts:

- It has blurred the artificial divide that sometimes existed between social affairs and economic affairs. (Social and labour affairs were often put in a box and ignored.)
- The ILO has begun co-operating with other international organisations to explain and promote its role as the organisation that sets international labour standards and promotes fundamental rights in the workplace.
- The policy issues we are dealing with such as the social clause and codes of conduct are not exclusive to the ILO, they are springing up in all international organisations and business needs a consistent and coherent input.

The IOE has therefore had to explain new fields of operation, working with organisations where we previously had no contact, such as the WTO

With globalisation it has become clear that business accepts that there is a role for an organisation like the ILO which is dedicated to promoting the "social rules of the game". The arrival of the new ILO Director-General, Juan Somavia was therefore viewed as a very positive development. We are now working on an agenda for change that will increase the relevance of the ILO to the business community and also provide a real forum to discuss the implications of social and labour dimensions of globalisation. Our key policy objectives for work in the ILO include:

- More focus on enterprise and enterprise development
- A less hysterical approach to the issue of trade and labour standards
- A review of the ILO's standard setting activities.

The debate on the future of ILO standard-setting will be the litmus test as to whether the ILO is to regain credibility, both with the business community and the various international institutions. We believe that the ILO is harming its credibility by continuing to adopt Conventions that are increasingly less ratified. The IOE and its members believe that there is a role for international labour standards, that is clear. But they should be ones that are relevant and meaningful and ultimately ratifiable for the majority of the ILO's member states.

The challenge for the IOE is to persuade its members that the ILO is changing and that their continued input is needed to effect that change. This is indeed a real challenge. Employers' organisations themselves are changing. Members now demand more in terms of service for their membership fee. The changing nature of industrial relations systems also means that some companies are less committed to automatically funding membership organisations than before. At the national level some organisations are concentrating on "core activities" and the axe often falls on international affairs in this process. This is indeed a paradox: at a time when international issues in their various forms have more potential than ever before to impact on companies whatever their size and wherever they operation, the temptation is to ignore. The challenge for the IOE is therefore demanding: to continue to explain the need to its members for a strong representative voice of business at international level on the one hand and to provide a coherent voice in the various mushrooming debates on labour and social affairs at the international level at the other.

Dan Cunniah

6. THE CHALLENGES FACING TRADE UNIONS IN THE 21st CENTURY*

1. INTRODUCTION

The accelerating globalisation of the economy characterised by the expansion of world trade in goods and services, international capital movements, including foreign investment, the inter-connection of financial markets and the growing share of multinational enterprises in total economic activity has brought the problems of human insecurity, unemployment and marginalisation to the top of the political agenda in many industrialised as well as developing countries. There is a growing realisation that the free market by itself cannot solve these problems Therefore the international trade union movement must reexamine its priorities, its strategies and structures in order to tackle the enormous problems placed before us by globalisation.

Trade unions have a vision of what the world should be like in the 21st century. A world free from poverty and oppression, where democracy extends from the workplace to the centres of political and economic power. A peaceful world where social justice, equality between women and men, and human rights prevail, and where discrimination is a thing of the past. Trade unions want decent work for all.

Can this vision become a reality? Our answer is yes and we believe that the international free trade union movement is a force that can make it happen.

We know what our movement can achieve by looking back at the first fifty years of the ICFTU's work. The generations that founded and built the ICFTU into the strong and globally representative organisation it is today also had a vision not dissimilar to ours. They faced what seemed at times to be insurmountable challenges but they changed the course of world history. They would not be satisfied with the world today, but they could be immensely proud of the progress working people have made in so much of the world through free trade unionism.

Tomorrow's challenges are very different from those of even the recent past. We

---

*   This lecture was based on a document prepared for the 17th World Congress of the ICFTU held in Durban, South Africa, in April, 2000.

R. Blanpain and C. Engels (eds), The ILO and the Social Challenge of the 21st Century, 65–74.
© 2001 *Kluwer Law International. Printed in Great Britain.*

know we must refashion our movement to achieve our goals. We must convince working women and men that by joining a union they can help to change their own lives for the better and those of people just like themselves in other countries. We must concentrate on successful strategies both to realise the aspirations of union members and to sustain a powerful and effective trade union movement. We must win acceptance world-wide of organised labour's right to influence programmes and policies. We must mobilise unions' capacity to achieve a balance of power on the international stage at the same time as making our presence felt at workplaces all over the world. The ICFTU must provide leadership to the free, democratic and independent trade unions of the world.

The tasks of the international trade union movement today are:

- *Extending democracy* at the workplace by asserting the right to organise and bargain for better conditions.
- *Reaching out* to the workers in the informal sector and to all those who currently have no voice and face discrimination and injustice, encouraging them to form and join unions and to achieve an end to discrimination.
- *Speaking out* for working women and men in the institutions of power of the new global economy, the multinationals and the intergovernmental organisations like the IMF, World Bank and WTO.
- *Strengthen our movement* to meet the changing needs of working families and the new forms and patterns of employment that globalisation and regional integration are creating.

2. WINNING RESPECT FOR THE RIGHT TO ORGANISE

Trade unions must assert and defend basic human rights at work everywhere, especially freedom of association. We must use these rights to bring new members into our unions and give them a voice on the things that really matter in their lives. And we must demonstrate that workplace democracy is a vital component in a new global system of ground rules for socially, economically and environmentally sustainable development.

The ICFTU will vigorously assert the basic internationally accepted human right to freedom of association defined in the ILO standards, especially Conventions 87 and 98. We will call on all member states of the ILO to account for their obligation to ensure that law and practice provide working women and men with the right to form and join unions and be protected from acts of anti-union discrimination. We will make full use of the ILO Declaration on Fundamental Principles and Rights at Work and its follow up adopted at the 1998 International Labour Conference which has reinforced the ILO's mandate as the international guarantor of the right to organise and other basic worker rights.

The ICFTU will continue to strengthen its ability to quickly and widely publicise attacks on union rights wherever they occur. We will also improve our capacity to translate this information into direct pressure on offending governments. We will also hold employers responsible for violations of these rights inside their enterprises and throughout their chains of production and service. Through our Annual Survey of Violations of Trade Union Rights and other efforts, we will work with affiliates, regional organisations, the ITS and human rights non-governmental organisations to make sure that abusers of trade union rights are named and shamed. We will demand that other governments and the business community use all available diplomatic, political and, if necessary, economic means to isolate governments that persistently and grossly abuse union rights.

Workers need a stronger ILO. Too often governments get away for years with ignoring increasingly strident criticisms of existing laws and recommendations for reform by the ILO's supervisory bodies. Where unions are barred from speaking and acting to find solutions to workers' fears and aspirations, social problems worsen and can ultimately undermine economic and political stability and peace with damaging consequences for neighbouring countries and the legitimacy of international rules aimed at increasing trade and investment. The ILO's authority must be buttressed by a new and more coherent system of multilateral support for fundamental workers rights. The ICFTU, through the Workers' Group, will fight to defend and enhance the work of the ILO.

3. REACHING OUT TO THE UNORGANISED

The ICFTU is convinced by the lessons of its own history that where working women and men are able to join unions without fear of reprisals they will want to combine together and seek a voice on their conditions of work and life. Even where the basic human right to freedom of association is not fully respected courageous women and men have built unions in the face of huge obstacles.

Organising is a continuous activity for unions that must always reflect the needs of people in different work situations and communities. But the rapid changes in the world of work demand global strategies to make union representation the natural choice for women and men.

This means mobilising and preparing millions of volunteers to take the union message to their friends and colleagues at work and sign them up into union member-ship. Key target groups are women, youth and informal sector workers.

• The ICFTU will work together with the Interrnational Trade Secretariats to strengthen support for affiliates' organising activities drawing on the wealth of experience from unions all over the world to back up union activists.

In an ever more interdependent world, new groups of union members need not only the backing of established unions in their own country but also from unions in other countries who face the same employers. Chains of production stretch from the shop-ping centres of the industrial world to small workshops in developing countries. Our aim is to connect workers through out the global chains of production by enlarging union co-operation.

- The ICFTU will work with the International Trade Secretariats to develop our collaboration with community groups and non-governmental organisations that share our principles. And we will demand that the international companies that drive so much of the global economy live up to their professions of good corporate world citizenship.

A further challenge for unions in the twenty first century is to organise the increasingly large numbers of workers in the large and expanding informal sector who have no formal employer. Governments are unable or unwilling to protect workers in large areas of economic activity as the informalisation of work continues. Hundreds of millions of working women and men in the developing world survive, often barely, outside the rules of employment law. Some are independent artisans, farmers and traders; others are employed by small unregistered businesses. Similarly in industrialised countries an increasing number of people are self-employed or contract workers, often in effect working for their former "employers", but with a legal status that effectively excludes them from all or most of the protections of employment laws.

The reality is that such workers need legal protections, social security, and a collective voice to represent their interests and engage in the struggle for improved living and working conditions. Efforts may need to extend to building collective institutions in addition to unions such as co-operatives, insurance schemes and credit unions.

- The ICFTU will act to address the problems faced by workers in the informal sector. We will work with the ILO, and international development agencies to assist and encourage affiliated organisations to help working people in the large and ever increasing informal sector. We will campaign for the right to organise of informal sector workers and develop a special programme to identify and spread the lessons of the most successful unions representing such workers. We will seek to establish pilot projects on effective organising approaches and help trade unions share experiences on how to achieve the protection of workers who are left unprotected because labour legislation is inadequate or not applied.

4. Mobilising for Equality at Work

Workers everywhere want fair treatment at work and in society. The fight to overcome discrimination in all its many forms is bringing millions of workers into our movement, notably women. Women are changing the face of our movement, bringing new energy and ideas to attack injustices old and new. But the pace of change within trade unions must accelerate. Unions cannot credibly lead the campaign for equality in the world of work if they themselves do not practise what they preach.

- The ICFTU will work to ensure that every affiliate has a plan of action for gender equality within the union movement, that all policies and programmes include a gender dimension and that union structures from top to bottom are opened up to women's' participation.

Women are joining the world's workforce at an accelerating pace but mostly at the bottom in low paid, low status, precarious jobs. The economic and social cost of discrimination, particularly against women but also on the grounds of race, colour, creed, political opinion, sexual orientation, disability and age, is incalculable. Unions are fighting discrimination because it is wrong but we are also convinced that promoting equality benefits the whole of society by releasing the productive potential of people who are unfairly denied decent work.

- The ICFTU will step up its campaign to ensure that the interests of working women are fully reflected in the development of a new framework of international rules for the global economy, building on the 1995 UN Beijing Platform for Action.
- The ICFTU will also strive to make sure action to overcome discrimination at work – including against migrants or on the basis of race, colour or national extraction – is given the highest political commitment and the financial resources to match. And the ICFTU will lead by example, acting as a catalyst for change in the trade union movement, to promote solidarity in diversity, as all workers must have their place in our organisations.

5. CAMPAIGNING FOR DECENT WORK FOR ALL

Working women and men join unions because they want decent and productive work, in conditions of freedom, equity, security and human dignity. In the twenty first century the struggle to obtain decent work for all will have an important global dimension. It is the task of the ICFTU to express these demands in the institutions of international power.

One of those institutions is the International Labour Organisation, the only international body where people are represented not just by governments but by employers and trade unions too. It has adopted "decent work for all" as its mission in the new millennium.

- The ICFTU will work to strengthen affiliates' efforts to make an impact on their governments' policies towards the IMF and World Bank, in order to build a strong social component to the emerging rules for governing the global economy. This requires an enhanced role for the ILO as an equal partner with bodies such as the IMF, World Bank and WTO in a cohesive economic and social strategy for sustainable development.

Liberalisation of capital and investment flows is creating a global market. Unions understand the potential of an integrated world economy for releasing innovation, growth in employment and the reduction of poverty but also know that the market does not discern the difference between employment and exploitation nor does it clean up after itself unless compelled to do so by government. Without strong co-ordinated government action, markets create damaging instability and inequality and, ultimately, destroy themselves.

The ICFTU firmly believes that a new social and economic architecture for sustainable global development is essential. Governments of many different political colours from all parts of the world know it too. Even big business is aware that the current system needs large-scale reform.

A substantial number of low income countries, especially in Africa, are mired in an unending burden of debt servicing, undermining any prospects for poverty eradication and sustainable growth. A new approach to development must incorporate the objectives of timely and comprehensive debt relief for poor countries which respect human rights.

Working women and men need a voice in the design of the new architecture at the global level and they need rights and representation at the work place where the forces of globalisation have a direct impact on their lives. The ICFTU has a responsibility to give voice to their concerns and to defend their interests.

Our firm conviction is that new global rules must guarantee fundamental workers' rights everywhere and that without this foundation multilateral institutions will have little political legitimacy and be unable to develop the authority needed to regulate the global market fairly and consistently.

The multilateral institutions are answerable to governments and the ICFTU must further develop its capacity to co-ordinate sustained pressure on governments for reform. Our work since the 1996 Congress is having some results. The issue of how to ensure a system wide support for the ILO's fundamental workers rights conventions is on the agenda of other international institutions. The ILO itself is developing a new vigour with its "decent work for all" mandate and raising its profile in the international policy making arena.

But still more must be done to explain and convince governments that unions have a constructive role to play in a global economy and that respect for basic workers' rights are as important as measures to protect foreign direct investment or the stability of the banking system.

- The ICFTU will therefore continue to press for the inclusion of respect for basic workers' rights in the multilateral trade system administered by the WTO alongside measures to increase the opening of markets to developing country exports.
- We will continue to campaign for a major programme of development assistance focussed on poverty reduction and a social development strategy built on the Copenhagen Commitments, including through our support to the successful outcome of the UN Special Sessions on gender equality and on social development in June 2000 and the UN Special Session on human settlements in 2001.

- We will renew our action for fundamental reforms of international finance markets to prevent crises such as that which hit Asia and many other countries in 1997 and 1998 and which is far from over for workers and their families.
- We will push for a formal requirement for the IMF, the World Bank and the regional development banks to recognise the importance of basic workers' rights and to undertake to promote those rights.
- We will increase our efforts to bring about a quick and large reduction of the debt burden of least developed countries which respect human rights, including fundamental workers' rights, and give priority to social spending.
- We will extend our campaign to abolish child labour building on our success in winning a new ILO Convention on the Worst Forms of Child Labour.
- We will increase our efforts to focus attention on the fight for safe working conditions and an employment dimension to environmental policies.
- And we will press governments and international organisations to target the creation of employment, especially for youth, in a co-ordinated strategy for high and stable growth of the world economy.

6. BUILDING PARTNERSHIPS TO MAKE MULTINATIONALS ACCOUNTABLE

Multinationals come in many shapes and sizes but workers' representatives everywhere have one common problem; finding the boss who really decides what happens to their work. Trade unions deal with many sorts of multinationals, good and bad. But even where companies accept unions, local representatives rarely get the sort of information they need to see how their subsidiary fits into the global reach of the company. This undermines the development of a constructive dialogue about where the company is planning to go and how this will impact on the lives of the people it employs and their communities.

- The ICFTU will enhance its co-operation with International Trade Secretariats to bring together union representatives throughout the major multinationals with the goal of establishing dialogue with management at the highest level.

The starting point of union strategies on multinationals is to strengthen the links between unions in different countries who share the same employer. Part of this work is the preparation and organisation of international union company councils. But occasional meetings will not be enough. We need to make full use of information technologies to exchange information and ideas on a systematic basis, especially at critical times like the preparation of organising or bargaining campaigns when international solidarity action may be needed.

- The ICFTU will co-operate with ITS developing global solidarity networks of unions inside multinationals.

Most big multinationals have a relationship with unions somewhere in their global operations. But there are many gaps. Connecting established unions with workers trying to organise in another country is an important challenge for the international trade union movement.

- The ICFTU will support ITS efforts to extend union representation in the multinationals and to put pressure on companies to adopt an open and constructive response to unions wherever they operate.

One important spin-off of globalisation is increasing concern amongst consumers, especially the young, about the working conditions of the people who make the products they buy. The ICFTU which represents 123 million workers all over the world can claim to represent at least three times that number of consumers because workers and their families are also consumers. This is a force to be reckoned with. The ICFTU will harness this force to put pressure on multinational companies to respect core labour standards everywhere.

The same powerful new mediums for advertising also expose the hypocrisy of some companies' claims to be good global citizens. The rapid growth of corporate codes of conduct in the last 5–10 years demonstrates that social responsibility is now an important part of the marketing strategy of many multinationals. However, too many codes are designed by public relations departments to hide rather than reveal the reality of working conditions in subsidiaries, suppliers and contractors.

- The ICFTU will continue to work with ITS to press companies and industry associations to ensure that their codes are consistent with the international core labour standards of the ILO and include systems for effective monitoring and independent verification. Our goal is codes to help ensure that all workers in multinationals and throughout their chains of production are free to chose to join unions and set their own working conditions through collective bargaining. The ICFTU will also continue to work with TUAC and the ITS to strengthen the OECD Guidelines for Multinational Enterprises and the ILO Tripartite Declaration on Multinational Enterprises and Social Policy. These instruments, with better implementation, can provide the means for governments as well as unions to have a positive influence on corporate behaviour. The ICFTU should work with TUAC and ITS to assess any new proposals for a multilateral framework for investment against the criteria of the contribution it would make to socially sustainable development. The ICFTU will promote the establishment and use of negotiated international framework agreements between companies and unions on workers' rights as an additional means of promoting trade union and workers' rights.

Moreover, the trade union movement is engaging in the UN Global Compact not as an alternative to rules and regulations for the global market, but because we believe that no matter how good and comprehensive such rules may become, there is a need for voluntary, private initiatives. At the national level, social partnership has proven to be a flexible and dynamic complement to legal frameworks which protect fundamental rights and labour standards. The ICFTU believes that international policy making would benefit from global dialogue between business and labour as well as with NGO's and other elements of civil society.

The UN and the international trade union movement, following a meeting on 20 January, 2000, issued a joint statement on the Global Compact which says "It was agreed that global markets required global rules. The aim should be to enable the benefits of globalisation increasingly to spread to all people by building an effective framework of multilateral rules for a world economy that is being transformed by the globalisation of markets."

7. CHANGING OURSELVES TO CHANGE THE WORLD

Trade unions the world over are living through a period of revolutionary change. Many of the workers in industries that formed the core of our movement are losing their jobs. New occupations are growing and are based on smaller more dispersed work units. Many men and women who previously had secure employment contracts now find themselves in precarious jobs with few legal rights of redress if they are badly treated. Massive numbers of working women and men in the developing world are struggling to survive in the jungle that is termed the informal sector.

- The ICFTU will undertake activities, campaigning and work with other organisations to help trade unions organise workers in the informal sector and enlarge the scope of protection of such workers.

We have to strengthen the trade union movement to meet the enormous challenges working women and men face in the era of globalisation.

As trade unions come to grips with globalisation, they are realising that international and national policies and actions are closely linked. Trade unions in nearly all countries and sectors are struggling to maintain their membership, showing the need for the ICFTU to focus the use of its resources ever more effectively. The ICFTU should encourage maximum co-operation, including joint activities and campaigns, with the ITS, and regional organisations. The partnership of the ICFTU and the ITS should facilitate building and mobilising effective international trade union solidarity to deliver for workers engaged in the struggle for their rights with governments and companies. It should also help to encourage national affiliates to incorporate trade union globalisation into all relevant aspects of their work..

- The ICFTU and ITS, working in partnership, must remain ready to respond in times of crisis, but we should also work with our respective affiliates to ensure that an international dimension is an integral part of national union strategies.

Building a more effective system of international response to the needs of affiliates requires increased co-operation between international trade union organisations. This will require an examination of the structures of international trade unionism that encompasses the ICFTU and its regional organisations, ITS, TUAC, the ETUC and national centres as well as other international and regional trade union bodies. This should build upon existing commitments including the strengthening of regional organisations and the deepening of the partnership with ITS. The current pace of globalisation and its harsh impact on the trade union position in the regions make it essential to further increase the ICFTU's capacity to pursue its policies, strategies and programmes including through more direct and efficient action by affiliates and at the level of the regional organisations. The ICFTU also needs to develop and encourage international union co-operation as a counterpart to regional economic co-operation agreements. It should further promote co-operation with other national, regional and international trade union organisations which pursue the same principles and objectives in this domain.

- The ICFTU will therefore invite the organisations of the international trade union movement to join a process of review with the objective of identifying how to help build stronger and more effective trade union solidarity.

We also need to look at how we work with non-governmental organisations that share our vision at the global, regional and national levels with a view to increasing the influence and effectiveness of the policies and work of the free, independent and democratic trade union movement. The ICFTU is already working closely with the International Cooperative Alliance (ICA) and some major NGOs working in the field of human rights such as Amnesty International, Human Rights Watch and the World Organisation Against Torture.

- The international trade union movement as a whole should continue to strengthen its capacity to campaign effectively for the realisation of our objectives, and to build international trade union solidarity through trade union education and information activities and through trade union development co-operation projects. The ICFTU will develop further its role as a focal point in the international free trade union movement for the exchange of information and technical and operational expertise amongst affiliates.

The challenge for the ICFTU is to reshape itself to help affiliates with the massive task of securing basic workers rights at the workplace, reaching out to the unorganised, making the union movement a focal point for the struggle against discrimination, social injustice, campaigning for decent work for all and getting the union voice heard in the international centres of private and public power.

A. Varkey Jose

7. THE FUTURE OF THE LABOUR MOVEMENT: SOME OBSERVATIONS ON DEVELOPING COUNTRIES

1. INTRODUCTION

Trade unions have been important institutions of industrial society; they have helped deliver significant outcomes in terms of improved living standards, equity and justice to workers all over the world. However, at the end of the twentieth century, unions face a situation marked by the universal trend towards greater liberalisation of economic and political regimes. The changing environment requires new approaches and strategies on the part of unions if they are to remain major social actors contributing to dynamic and equitable growth. It is argued in this note that liberalisation/ globalisation, which brings formidable challenges to unions, also provides them with opportunities to play a far more effective and politically important role in society.

This note reviews three sets of issues which should figure in a discussion of the changing role of trade unions. These are: (i) the traditional role of unions; (ii) the changing environment in the world of work and its impact on unions; and (iii) union responses in terms of new approaches and strategies. The different economic, political and geographic settings of unions around the world are given special attention.

The issues raised have been assembled with the following objectives: (i) to identify the gaps in knowledge concerning the responses of unions in different environments; (ii) to define an agenda for further research highlighting the contribution of labour and unions to society; and (iii) to set the terms for policy debates involving unions and researchers on promising approaches for the future.

The above objectives have been incorporated into a programme on "Organised labour in the 21st century", undertaken by the International Institute for Labour Studies of the International Labour Organisation. The issues listed above are being investigated within the framework of studies organised by the Institute in different countries. Based on the findings of these studies, which are at various stages of completion, this paper discusses some questions relevant to the future of labour movements, with special reference to developing countries.[1]

R. Blanpain and C. Engels (eds), The ILO and the Social Challenge of the 21st Century, 75–92.
© *2001 Kluwer Law International. Printed in Great Britain.*

2. THE ROLE OF TRADE UNIONS

Trade unions have traditionally performed three principal roles in their relations with individual employers, business associations, the State, and the public at large.

- The economic role of facilitating production and ensuring an equitable distribution of the value-added. This has been achieved mainly through collective bargaining and negotiations at enterprise level, industry/sector level or national level.
- The democratic and representative role of providing voice and identity to labour at the workplace, and in society at large. This includes: (a) representing workers in individual grievance procedures; (b) giving voice to labour's views on economic and social policies at all levels ncluding enterprises; and (c) promoting cooperation between capital and labour with a view to securing employment, improved working conditions and living standards consistent with sustainable growth.
- The social role of minimising the risk of exclusion in an industrial society by: (a) promoting solidarity among workers in different sectors and occupational groups; (b) providing special services to members of unions; and (c) serving as an anchor for broad-based social movements sharing similar values and goals.

2.1. Bargaining and Representation

The first and second functions roughly correspond to the two familiar roles of unions – negotiating on wages and working conditions, and representing workers' interests in various forums (Freeman and Medoff, 1984). The balance of these two functions has been influenced by the pace and spread of industrialisation over the past decades.

The experience of a number of industrialised countries suggests that, over a period of time, unions have grown from a predominantly bargaining role to a specialised role, representing the voice and interests of labour. This transition came with economic growth and a sustained increase in capital intensity both in product and labour markets. Unions served as a conduit for turning economic growth and prosperity into improved living standards for workers. The benefits of collective bargaining were transmitted to a broad spectrum of society in terms of wage and non-wage benefits, particularly through a reduction of working time. More importantly, unions helped maintain a wage structure which minimised income disparities between workers; in the process they managed to correct an imbalance in distribution which markets tended to create.

The post-war decades conditioned unions to function in a corporate environment, combining their traditional bargaining activities with the newly acquired voice and representation functions. Corporatism, which was originally a state-sponsored arrangement for cooperation between labour and capital, was transformed into societal corporatism from which social policies have been derived through democratic decision making (Crouch and Dore, 1990). Workers identified common ground and interests with employers and exercised a moderating influence on business strategies.

Together they developed labour policies which fitted in with the fluctuating fortunes of business. The new approach was particularly successful in countries like Japan where institutions governing industrial relations were modelled on those in industrialised Western countries.[2]

2.2. Social Cohesion

Unions nurtured social cohesion by involving themselves in the design of institutions which guaranteed a secure income and decent living standards in society as a whole. As industrialisation and economic growth led to major changes affecting the age, gender and skill composition of the workforce, a new range of issues emerged for consideration by the unions. Over the years, they embraced a broader agenda including health care, leisure, recreation, retirement and non-wage benefits from employment. They appeared on new representative bodies and platforms for dialogue, and decisively influenced the content of social policy.

The ILO studies, particularly those on Israel, Japan and Sweden, show that at an intermediate stage, unions rose to the challenge of meeting the changing requirements of an industrial society; established themselves as credible partners and provided a variety of services to members, including mutual aid, credit, insurance, housing and consumer services mostly through cooperatives linked to union membership (Nathanson et al. 1999; Inoue, 1999; and Fahlbeck, 1999). The Swedish study suggests that in Scandinavia the preeminent position which unions enjoyed in terms of membership and influence over public policies was anchored in the services which unions provided to their members. One of the oldest trade unions in the Middle East, the Histadrut of Israel, grew in strength until the early 1990s with an impressive membership tally based on the provision of services, notably health care which covered practically the entire population.

3. THE STRENGTH AND INFLUENCE OF TRADE UNIONS

The preceding discussion points to some tangible indicators of the strength and impact of unions which may be listed as follows: (a) union density – whether unions have built a solid base through membership of the workers they represent; (b) the capacity to mobilise – whether unions, irrespective of numerical strength, have the capacity to mobilise labour successfully; (c) labour institutions – whether the results of union action have been institutionalised through labour legislation, collective agreements, and union participation in the administration of benefits; and (d) union structures – whether unions have developed appropriate structures to deal with labour issues arising at local, regional and global level.

3.1. Union Density

The proportion of workers who belong to a union has been the most visible symbol of union strength. Right through the period of industrialisation in the developed countries, unions grew in strength, bringing nearly two-thirds of the labour force into their fold. This trend was reversed in the mid-1970s when union density dropped steeply in many industrialised countries. It has continued to increase in a number of developing countries, but at an extremely slow rate. There is considerable scope for growth in union membership among the developing nations, especially in the newly industrialising countries (ILO, 1997).

The growth of trade unions from the collective bargaining function towards a role dominated by voice and representation of workers, seems to have taken place against the background of high density unionism[3] which gained ground mainly in continental Europe and in Japan. The broad membership base which unions commanded and the equitable distribution which they promoted in major sectors and enterprises strengthened the position of unions, giving them more power to bargain or collaborate and to derive successful outcomes.

3.2. Mobilising Capacity

Apart from numerical strength the capacity to mobilise, which brings significant results for workers, is a direct measure of the degree of political support which unions enjoy. The experience of developed countries suggests that union capacity for mobilisation has a synergistic effect on the development of democracy. Unions have consolidated their political space and in the process they have strengthened the democratic institutions of such societies. As industrialisation spread, unions emerged as major partners influencing the allocation, stabilisation and redistribution functions of modern governments. As a result the post-war decades in Europe have been marked by the ascent of an activist State which supervises the distribution of benefits to workers and their dependents. Certain governments have mobilised resources in excess of 50 per cent of GDP in order to finance the welfare society (Esping-Anderson, 1996; Tanzi and Schuknecht, 1995).

3.3. Labour Institutions

Union capacity to deliver successful outcomes for labour means that the benefits they have won have to be incorporated in statutes governing the labour market. In industrialised countries, unions influenced the design and development of the post-war system of industrial relations which was based on a strong political commitment to full employment and workers' welfare. Some salient features of the system were: (a) participation in full-time employment, governed by an open-ended contract; (b) collectively negotiated wage structure with minimal dispersion across skill categories; (c) social benefits to workers and their dependents distributed through the main income earner; (d) control over working time and safety standards; and (e) job security for individual workers. As it happened, the industrial society with an egalitarian base, fostered by unions, became a powerful engine of growth and prosperity.

The institution of industrial relations was not unique to the developed countries.

Some variants emerged in developing countries too, albeit involving a smaller proportion of the total industrial workforce. In the aftermath of decolonisation, many States initiated development programmes and embarked on industrialisation based on import substitution strategies. The unions became major players, occupying a vantage position supported by State patronage. Regulated industries and public-sector enterprises, such as transport, communications and utilities, became a fertile ground for the growth of unions. In a few countries, such as India, where political pluralism and procedural democracy gained ground (Dahl, 1998), independent unions occupied a prominent place (Bhattacherjee, 1999).

Contractual laws and legal safeguards – mostly adapted from the industrialised countries – were established to fortify an incipient industrial society and to ensure the presence of a stable and committed labour force for the new urban industrial enclaves. Secure jobs, guaranteed higher wages and better working conditions were viewed as preconditions for the development of an industrial society. These provisions often became the critical elements of a "social compact" which set the terms of compromise between capital, labour and the State in sharing the national product (Webster and Adler, 1998). The compact worked in the early stages of industrialisation, but eventually it failed to take on board the concerns of a broad spectrum of workers in developing countries, where the labour institutions came to be viewed as problems rather than as solutions.

It is important to view the institutional safeguards for labour in a historical perspective, to assess their past contribution and evaluate their relevance to contemporary labour markets. The need arises because there are strident demands for the removal of these safeguards; it is argued that they protect the interests of workers, sometimes derisively referred to in developing countries as the labour aristocracy.[4]

3.4. Union Structures

Trade unions have adapted to the changing environment by creating new structures for organisation and interest representation. Some functions have been centralised and taken over by apex bodies while others have been decentralised to plant or enterprise level. Collective bargaining has been centralised at national or sectoral level with a view to deriving framework agreements for the entire economy or sector. The post-war decades witnessed the establishment of new institutions for labour/management cooperation. Enterprise unionism provided a platform to build on the macro-level framework agreements and to share the fruits of growth in an environment of cooperation.

The new structures for labour/management cooperation have been influenced by the economic and social environment of the countries or regions they belong to. In Japan, for example, such cooperation was built on the presence of "quasi-communities of labour" which adopted a problem-solving approach within enterprises. The quasi-communities helped develop a pattern of enterprise restructuring with flexible

79

employment practices based on retraining and relocation of workers and with minimal use of lay-offs (Inoue, 1999). The Works Councils, which started in countries like Germany, where labour and business practise mutually beneficial consultation (Rogers and Streeck, 1993), are now being adopted all over Europe.

4. THE CHANGING ENVIRONMENT

Recent decades have seen profound changes in the political and economic environment which have had a negative effect on the position and influence of trade unions. The interrelated factors which contributed to this situation may be listed as follows. First, globalisation has led to intense competitive pressure in product markets, accelerated the mobility of capital, and added to the vulnerability of labour. Second, technological changes have made it possible to reshape production through new forms of industrial organisation, including sub-contracting and the spatial reorganisation of production systems. Third, there are changes in the skill composition of the workforce along with large scale entry of women into labour markets.

There is a discernible trend towards enterprise downsizing and a shift in industrial employment away from large enterprises. This trend is connected with technological changes. The new units of production, each employing a smaller number of workers albeit with uniform skill endowments, tend to be geographically dispersed even outside the boundaries of urban labour markets.

The skill composition of workers is changing and they are increasingly differentiated by their competence. At the higher end of the scale, workers tend to be better educated, career minded, individualistic and less motivated by class interests and solidarity. On the other hand, there is a discernible concentration of workers at the lower end in service industries or occupations. Such workers tend to be either women or migrants.

Flexible labour market policies have gained legitimacy and political support in the climate of economic liberalism. Practices such as subcontracting, outsourcing and the hiring of temporary and part-time workers, long considered as atypical employment, are becoming more common, especially at the lower end of the labour market. The net outcome is an increased segmentation of labour markets.

In addition, the political environment which conditioned the early phase of industrial relations is undergoing change. The historical alliance between the labour movement and the social democratic regime of industrial countries has weakened over time. The pervasive presence of an activist State, committed to full employment and pursuing expansionary economic policies in both public and private sectors, did not continue beyond the 1970s. In contrast the State has been withdrawing from the domain of employment and income policies, and governments have been moving away from any direct involvement in the creation of jobs. The new policy emphasis is on the governance of institutions to ensure the functioning of markets.

The sections below briefly review the consequences for labour of the above changes in different national settings.

4.1. Unions in industrialised countries

There are indications of a qualitative transformation of labour relations in the industrialised countries, which may be listed as follows:

(a) *A new regime of decentralised production.* New enterprises are decentralised, small or medium-sized units of production where unions tend to enjoy greater autonomy in workplace negotiations. At macro-level, unions increasingly take responsibility for harmonising the interests of workers, and strive to achieve multi-employer agreements on minimum standards.

(b) *Changing labour–management relations.* Enterprise managers are turning to the development of human resources in preference to the conventional workplace management regimes preferred by unions. Human resource management policies are primarily addressed to skilled professionals and technicians at the higher end of the spectrum. Unions are adapting to the new structures, while maintaining their presence as a balancing force in the entire economy.

(c) *Regionalisation and trade unions.* The transnational mobility of capital and production has led to a consolidation of markets at regional level, as in the European Union and NAFTA. Other regional trading arrangements may evolve in future. The implications for income distribution within and across regions remain to be explored.

(d) *The rise of wage disparities.* The differentiation of workers based on widening skill gaps has weakened the solidarity platform of trade unions. Unions are under pressure to develop wage policies which accommodate productivity differentials for greater efficiency in resource allocation.

(e) *Unions as service providers.* Worker perceptions of union effectiveness were traditionally enhanced by the unions' role in administering active labour market policies and channelling benefits, such as skill upgrading, employment services, unemployment insurance, health care and pensions. Intense competition and the emphasis on privatisation seem to have undermined the status of unions as providers of vital services.[5]

(f) *Changing attitudes towards unions.* Worker commitment to unions appears to be weakening due to the rise of individualism. At the higher end of the skill spectrum, workers seem indifferent to a collective identity and are less dependent on unions. Their personal identity is defined less in terms of class and more in terms of social functions, autonomy and mobility.

4.2. Unions in Less Developed Countries

Globalisation has impacted on workers and their organisations in developing countries. Recent decades have witnessed a shift away from inward-looking industrialisation strategies, a break from paternalistic industrial relations, and a significant rise in labour militancy.

The build-up of competitive pressure in both domestic and external markets led to the adoption of liberal economic policies which were reflected in a move away from inward-looking industrialisation and protectionism towards export-oriented industries and free trade policies. The State progressively withdrew from production and invited private capital to enter spheres traditionally reserved for the public sector. The earliest manifestations of this shift were among the newly industrialising countries of East and Southeast Asia.

Among those countries, notably in the Republic of Korea, Malaysia and Singapore, the State assumed the role of guiding the course of economic development and adopting industrialisation strategies geared to export markets and foreign direct investment (Chang, 1994). Policy measures were designed to insulate these strategies from wage pressures and strikes. Legislation and executive action were preferred to collective bargaining. Official guidelines restrained the movement of wages, while transfers, promotions, lay-offs, retrenchment and job assignments were deemed to lie outside the scope of collective bargaining (Kuruvilla, 1996). Enterprise unionism, a role model from the developed countries, was encouraged as an appropriate forum for representing the interests of workers (Song, 1999).

Elsewhere in the developing world, liberal economic policies came to the fore in the mid-1980s. A mirror image of changes in the labour markets of industrialised countries associated with the adoption of liberal economic policies could be observed in the developing countries. Four elements have been pervasive in these countries: (a) the disintegration of large workplaces and the rise of smaller geographically dispersed units of production; (b) an outward expansion of the labour market beyond the boundaries of the urban sector; (c) a skill-based differentiation of the workforce and (d) a rise in significant wage disparities. These developments have implications for the strategies of workers and their unions.

An ominous outcome of the retreat of the State was the breakdown of the social pact which trade unions had taken for granted. In many developing countries unions organised huge protests which were not simply a response to the decline in material conditions, but a reaction against the breach of trust implicit in the collapse of the pact.[6] On the other hand, business leaders in the private sector made strident calls for the removal of protectionist legislation, which they believed was anachronistic and an impediment to industrial development.

The following paragraphs review the main challenges facing unions and their responses, mainly based on the evidence from case studies in developing countries. We then discuss some issues which are likely to figure on the union agenda in the coming decades.

5. UNIONS: CHALLENGE AND RESPONSE

In general, trade unions adapt their strategies to meet the requirements of constituents in a changing environment. Such adaptation means going beyond traditional demands centred on wages, working conditions, and non-wage benefits met mainly through organisation and collective representation. The relevant issues for consideration here are: whether unions have maintained their position with respect to traditional constituent demands; how they are adapting to the new environment by organising new constituents, addressing new concerns, developing new perspectives on their role in society, and enhancing their image as major social actors. The discussion is restricted to three sets of issues: (a) building the membership base; (b) changing the union structures; and (c) collective action for institutional benefits. The purpose is to highlight some strategic choices before unions in the newly industrialising and developing countries.

5.1. Membership Campaigns

Webster and Adler (1998) observe that unions all over the world are surrounded by greater liberalisation of economic and political regimes and that these two developments together hold out prospects for creating new rules of the game compelling key social actors – governments, organised labour, business and (in some cases) community organisations – to negotiate and conclude agreements on major economic and social policies. When social interests are mediated by democratic regimes there is an opportunity to resolve the tensions likely to arise in the course of economic liberalisation and to negotiate a compromise solution. The capacity of unions to influence the course of events, however, depends on their strength and support among the unionised and non-unionised sections of society.

Membership campaigns organised by unions may be viewed in relation to two target groups: the traditional and the non-traditional constituents. Traditional constituents are those in established union strongholds such as the public sector and labour-intensive industries, while non-traditional constituents are the new entrants to labour markets such as highly skilled professionals, white-collar workers, and casual workers in private-sector enterprises.

5.1.1. Strategies Towards Traditional Constituents
The position of unions among traditional members has been affected because the changing environment has eroded their position as key allies of the State. The global flight of capital and the decline or migration of specific industries have added to the growing vulnerability of labour. Privatisation, the downsizing of enterprises and the adoption of flexible employment practices have all affected the strength of unions in their traditional bastions.

Public employment policies are reaching a turning point. The capacity of the State for resource mobilisation and implicitly for job creation is being circumscribed and it is highly unlikely that public expenditure reaching 50 per cent of GDP will ever materialise in developing countries. Increasingly the State is moving away from any fiscal responsibility to manage the labour market from the demand side.

If unions are to build up their membership base in such an adverse environment they need to consider the special requirements of their traditional constituents, which are: (a) protection of employment, working conditions and social security; (b) training, human resource development and career mobility; and (c) provision of benefits, credit support, legal assistance and advisory services.

Unions have had some success in retaining members by promoting job security and upward mobility, and through channelling special benefits. This has been ensured through their participation in the administration of labour market policies and social security schemes (Nathanson et al., 1999; Wong, 1999). The role of unions in providing services such as skill improvement, unemployment insurance, social security and employment exchanges, have helped enhance workers' perception of union effectiveness and ensured their continued loyalty. It should be emphasised here that unions, in light of their experience in this field, have the potential to emerge as major development partners in society.

As the largest organised groups in developing societies, unions can make a unique contribution to the development community. They are directly involved with economic systems of production and distribution; they can influence the course and content of employment, social and economic policies; they are representative and accountable; they have considerable experience in organising the more vulnerable sections of society; and they have the experience and standing required to access national legal systems and public facilities. They can contribute through their long-standing relationships with such development institutions as consumer cooperatives, housing societies, health funds, and social security organisations. In order to make full use of this potential, however, unions need to tend their public image.

There is an important element of taking the public on board when unions want to emerge as a voice defending the rights and interests of their constituents. An exclusively economic platform on which workers interests are in conflict with those of society could be counterproductive. The convergence of members' interests which characterised industrial society no longer applies in the newly industrialising countries, where there is conspicuous individualism and divergence of interests.[7]

Technological innovation and rising productivity are causing major changes in traditional union strongholds, notably in public sector services.[8] There are compelling reasons for the public service industries to remain competitive, ostensibly through an increase in productivity. Unions need to work out new strategies to respond to the changing environment. More importantly, they need to secure a niche as efficient providers of services both to their constituents and to the public at large.

Furthermore, rising consumer sensitivities and recognition of the fact that the public are important consumers of services provided by the State and utility industries, are beginning to bear on union strategies. Industrial action in a public-service industry is likely to cost more in terms of popular support since the damage will probably, spread beyond the employers. The dilemma faced by unions in winning public support for industrial action has been highlighted in the ILO study on the Republic of Korea (Song, 1999).

5.1.2. Non-traditional Constituents
Non-traditional constituents may be grouped into several distinct, but overlapping categories: (i) new entrants at the higher end of labour markets, including professional

and white-collar workers; (ii) casual workers, who are either part-time or temporary; (iii) home-based workers and those in the informal sector; and (iv) women workers.

Two major groups of casual workers are part-timers and temporary workers. By and large, part-timers fall into two groups: (a) those with higher education and skills who choose to take qualitatively better jobs on a part-time basis; and (b) those with little education and few skills who are in low-paid jobs with limited career prospects. At the lower end of the skill spectrum, both part-timers and temporary workers are often young, women or migrant workers. Casual workers, in so far as they lack any long-term attachment to a single employer, tend to be disadvantaged in their access to the non-wage benefits which are usually linked to service in the same firm.

The informal sector has grown exponentially with an increasing share of new jobs either being created in, or outsourced to, the informal sector. Union strategies to bridge the gap between the formal and informal sectors are rapidly becoming central to the future of trade unions in these countries. The interests of workers in the two sectors are not necessarily antithetical. Several common elements and shared concerns bring them together and offer prospects for collective action (Sanyal, 1991). Members of low-income households in developing countries often work in both the formal and informal sectors. Low-income workers from both sectors often live in the same neighbourhood, and have similar civic and community needs. These commonalities provide some basis for union-led action.

Increasingly, the typical worker is no longer a male breadwinner supporting a dependent family. Currently there are more women in the labour force belonging to either two-earner or even single-earner households. The growth of a predominantly female labour force is built on activities which are part-time, temporary or home-based, thereby accentuating inequalities in the labour markets. In developing countries, the influx of women workers has mostly been towards insecure and poorly paid types of work.[9]

The concentration of workers at the lower end of the labour market, especially in service industries and occupations, provides unions with a unique opportunity to build a new constituency. There have recently been encouraging union initiatives to organise new members and create suitable structures to represent their interests (Sanyal, 1991; Bhattacherjee, 1999). However, no major breakthrough or conspicuous gains have been reported in this field. In light of the available evidence one can only surmise that organising non-traditional members will be the main concern of trade unions in developing countries.[10]

5.2. *Trade union structures*

The new economic environment requires a reorganisation of trade union structures, which may be assessed by the following indicators: (i) decentralisation and adaptation of unions to new forms of industrial organisation; (ii) creation of new union structures to ensure representation of workers in the spatially decentralised units of production;

(iii) measures to ensure the financial viability of unions which take on new responsibilities to provide services to the members, and (iv) centralisation and/or coordination of union functions through mergers or alliances at national or sectoral level. We focus on the first two indicators mentioned above, since they are given more attention in the studies.

5.2.1. Decentralised Bargaining

The case studies reviewed here suggest that among the newly industrialised and developing countries, differentiation of the workforce and reorganisation of production processes have led to the rise of bargaining in the decentralised units of production. This corresponds to experience in the industrialised countries, when unions increasingly took on a voice and representative function within the framework of company unions and Works Councils.

As the benefits from liberalised economic regimes filtered down to employees at the higher end of the skill spectrum, the orientation of workers shifted to economic issues. One discernible outcome was a gradual decline in radical political unionism and a rise in economic unionism demanding improved benefits at enterprise level. The new structures offered efficient solutions; they delivered better wages and fringe benefits, albeit to a smaller group, compared to the previous structures which had catered to larger numbers in an environment of greater militancy and class solidarity.

The rise of decentralised bargaining in India is associated with the rise of independent company unions which are not necessarily affiliated to apex bodies or political parties. From the 1980s onwards, independent unions pursuing decentralised bargaining became distinct entities in India, whereas they were already present in the newly industrialised countries of East and Southeast Asia (Song, 1999; Bhattacherjee, 1999). It has also been noted that the rise of decentralised bargaining and independent unions was associated with greater regional disparities in income distribution.[11]

A distinct feature of the situation in India, as well as in other developing countries, is the divergence of interests between the two extremes of a vastly polarised labour force. This makes it difficult for unions to combine traditional wage bargaining with their new role of giving voice and representation to workers at plant level. The first is a political task. The Indian experience suggests that the voice function is increasingly moving out of the domain of politically affiliated unions. The prolific growth of company unions which are not affiliated to political parties is a case in point (Bhattacherjee, 1999).

5.2.2. Union Structures at the Lower End

Decentralised and geographically dispersed units of production are not necessarily viable in terms of size and location for the purpose of unionising workers. There is an inverse relationship between the cost of unionisation and the size of enterprises which warrants a fresh look at organisational structures that can maximise the benefits of unionisation.

What is the nature of the structure which can bring spatially dispersed smaller units into the union fold? Can workers be unionised on the basis of their enterprise identity which could be affiliated to a sectoral or industry-based union? What should be the preferred mode of representation at enterprise level? Should there be a single union representing the majority of workers or should there be multiple unions representing different interest groups which might overlap with occupational groups? Can workers be unionised on the basis of their occupational identity? These vital issues, which impinge on the future of trade unions, are currently being discussed in the policy forums of many developing countries.

A review of union structures in developing countries, notably India, suggests a tendency to separate the bargaining and voice functions; this has major implications for future union strategies. A logical outcome of any separation of the bargaining and voice functions is a further deterioration in income distribution. That does not augur well for unions, or for developing countries. Any society which harbours deep inequalities in income distribution tends to limit the functioning of redistributive institutions. Trade unions in such societies might not be able to perform their role as the purveyors of social cohesion. In terms of future union strategies, this implies a serious effort to prevent any deterioration of income inequalities in developing countries.

In the rest of this paper we look at some union strategies which could prevent an aggravation of income inequalities.

5.3. Collective action and institutional benefits

Union capacity to deliver successful outcomes depends on whether workers' rights and interests have been incorporated into legislation or other regulatory instruments of the labour market. As for building institutional capacity, the following objectives have been prominent on the agenda of unions: (i) legislative provisions guaranteeing job security, unemployment insurance, and special benefits on termination of employment; and social security providing for health care and pension schemes; (ii) multi-employer agreements on employment, wages, working conditions, hours of work, and non-wage benefits of workers; (iii) ability to influence economic and social policies through consultation and dialogue with employers and public authorities.

Labour legislation, collective agreements, social security and minimum wages already in place are clear indicators of the strength and influence of trade unions. They reflect a capacity to influence public opinion and mobilise action in support of the demands of their constituents. In developing countries, notably in Asia, unions have had significant achievements in maintaining or upgrading statutory safeguards on employment and working conditions. Nonetheless, such gains are mostly restricted to workers in the formal sector.

A politically important task for unions is to build distributive institutions to defend the interests of workers at the lower end of the market, particularly the vast reservoir of workers in the informal sector. Ideally this could be attained through macro-level framework agreements encompassing minimum standards of employment, minimum wage, portable benefits including health care and safety nets which workers are entitled to irrespective of the location of employment. The question is whether unions can empower themselves to guarantee a secure income and decent working conditions for all. Such empowerment is a precondition for unions to emerge as credible partners ensuring social cohesion.

Two significant observations emerge from the studies reviewed; they also point to the tasks ahead and help us define the content of union strategies in the coming decades. First, unions are faced with rising income inequalities in developing societies and therefore should focus more on strategies to prevent any further deterioration. Second, union success in safeguarding the rights and interests of workers has come through their participation in democratic institutions. Therefore, it is only through strengthening these institutions that unions can consolidate their gains.

5.4. Correcting Inequalities

It is time the concerns of the lower tiers of the workforce figured prominently on the agenda for collective bargaining. In practical terms unions should aim at securing a minimum income for all in the labour market. The means of action should be through establishing minimum standards on employment, wages, working conditions and social security, and also ensuring universal access to these standards.

Trade unions are ideally placed to lead an initiative for a *social minimum wage*, consisting of the right to income security and other entitlements such as education, health, shelter and a safe environment. The exact nature of such entitlements could be decided at societal level through agreements on redistributive transfers involving the social partners. Transfers aimed at meeting the basic needs of the population can help set the "reserve price of labour" at a politically acceptable level, which cannot be undermined by market forces.[12]

The above approach to setting wages through redistributive transfers is significantly different from the conventional approach to fixing minimum wages through administered prices. Here the emphasis is on the political process which requires political parties to enter the field and organise the unorganised around a redistributive agenda. Only political democratisation with a strong emphasis on mobilising low-income groups would make the social minimum wage a reality in developing countries. This takes us to an even more important item on the union agenda i.e. strengthening democracy and human rights in developing countries.

5.5. Building Democratic Institutions

One lesson emerging from the experience of unions in industrialised countries is that civil and political liberties are essential preconditions for exercising labour rights, and that only a liberal democracy can provide the institutional environment for fulfilling these rights. Many developing countries correspond to the rudimentary stages in the evolution of democratic institutions. In a number of these countries trade unions have been instrumental in accelerating the pace of transformation through their sustained support and solidarity with the struggle for liberal democracy. Only prolonged struggle and profound sacrifice have brought them closer to the goal of guaranteeing civil and political liberties to a broad spectrum of society.

The Republic of Korea is a clear example of unions transforming their initial organising space into political space and decisively influencing the transition to democracy. Such transition was the culmination of a series of events, most notably the struggle to revive democratic institutions against an authoritarian regime. Democratisation led to new union structures, the organisation of new groups, multiple unionism and new political affiliations. Securing legal status for unions, particularly white-collar unions and industrial unions, was a significant achievement of the Korean labour movement. Similarly, the rise of multiple unions associated with political parties in a pluralist environment is a recent development (Song, 1999). The parallel development of democracy and trade unions in the Republic of Korea only underscores the synergy and strength the two institutions can derive from each other.

More importantly, the experience of East Asia is likely to be repeated in other countries. In this scenario trade unions would eventually lead the way to a constitutionally liberal society in which civil and political liberties, including the right to life, property and freedom of expression, become accessible to all citizens. This goal also implies a long and difficult journey ahead for the unions, as many developing societies are far from any constitutional guarantee of civil liberties. In such situations, it is the workers, notably migrants, minorities, those in the informal sector and in rural labour markets, who bear the brunt of human rights violations.

Trade unions, as representatives of a very organised and articulate group in society, have a historic mandate to defend and promote human rights. To achieve this, unions need to move beyond their customary role of defending civil and political rights as the basis of labour rights, and enter the broader terrain of defending economic and social rights. Union priorities in this field include appropriate human rights programmes in collaboration with other actors in society.

Here we come to the strategic importance of unions building alliances and coalitions between the partners in civil society with a view to building support for a human rights agenda. Such coalitions among interest groups in pursuit of common goals and shared values are absolutely essential for unions to fulfil their historic mission of maintaining social cohesion.

The value of collective action pioneered by unions as a means of attaining common objectives is widely recognised by a broad spectrum of interest groups. At the same time, unions themselves are entering partnerships or strategic alliances with other actors in civil society, including gender groups, cooperatives, community associations, human rights bodies, consumers and environmental groups. Often they require trade unions to transcend the boundaries of the workplace and address the concerns of communities, ethnic groups, religious organisations and neighbourhood associations.

The preceding discussion concerning the priorities of the labour movement in developing societies may be summed up as follows. A politically important option in the coming decades will be to build on its established role in safeguarding social cohesion. This implies a strategic orientation to the long-term goals of security, equity and justice for all in the world of work. The above goals are attainable through redistributive transfers, specifically aimed at correcting income inequalities and raising the level of social consumption. The strategies for reaching the goals need to be anchored in the mobilisation of diverse interest groups in society on a political platform. An enduring niche for the labour movement in developing societies means a relentless pursuit of the redistributive agenda.

BIBLIOGRAPHY

Bezuidenhout, A. 1999. "Towards Global Social Movement Unionism? Trade Union Responses to Globalization: A Case Study of South Africa", draft, International Institute for Labour Studies (Geneva, ILO).

Bhattacherjee, D. 1999. *Organized labour and economic liberalization – India: Past, present and future*, Discussion Paper, Labour and Society Programme, International Institute for Labour Studies (Geneva, ILO).

Bronfenbrenner, K.; Friedman,S.; Hurd, R.; Oswald, R.; Seeber, R. (eds). 1998. *Organizing to win, New research on union strategies* (Ithaca and London ILR Press, Cornell University Press).

Chang, Ha-Joon. 1994. "State interventions and structural change" in *Structural Change and Economic Dynamics*, Vol 5, No. 2 (Oxford University Press).

Crouch, C.; Dore, R. 1990. "Whatever happened to corporatism?" in *Corporatism and Accountability* (Oxford, Clarendon Press).

Dahl, R. A. 1998. *On Democracy* (New Haven, Yale University Press).

Dovydeniene, R. 1999. *Trade union response to globalization in Lithuania*, Discussion Paper, Labour and Society Programme, International Institute for Labour Studies (Geneva, ILO).

Esping-Anderson, G. 1996. "After the golden age? Welfare state dilemmas in a global economy" in Esping-Anderson (ed). *Welfare states in transition, national adaptations in global economies* (London, Sage).

Fahlbeck, R. 1999. *Trade Unions in Sweden*, Discussion Paper, Labour and Society Programme, International Institute for Labour Studies (Geneva, ILO).

Freeman, R.; Medoff, J. 1984. *What do Unions Do?* (New York, Basic Books).

Inoue, S. 1999. *Japanese trade unions and their future: Opportunities and challenges in an era of globalization*, Discussion Paper, Labour and Society Programme, International Institute for Labour Studies (Geneva, ILO).

International Labour Office. 1997. *World Labour Report 1997–98: Industrial relations, democracy and social stability* (Geneva, ILO).

Jose. A. V. 1994. "Social policy towards wage determination: Some lessons from the Indian States", *Abstracts of The International Congress on Kerala Studies* (AKG Centre for Research and Studies, Thiruvananthapuram).

Kuruvilla, S. 1996. "Linkages between industrialization strategies and industrial relations/human resource policies: Singapore, Malaysia, the Philippines and India", in *Industrial and Labour Relations Review*, Vol 49, No. 4 (Ithaca, N.Y., Cornell University).

Nathanson, R. et al. 1999. *Union response to a changing environment: The New Histadrut – The General Federation of Labour in Israel*, Discussion Paper, Labour and Society Programme, International Institute for Labour Studies (Geneva, ILO).

Rogers, J.; Streeck, W. (eds.) 1993. "The study of works councils: concepts and problems", in *Works Councils – Consultation, Representation, and Cooperation in Industrial Relations* (National Bureau of Economic Research Cooperative Labour Market Series).

Rogers, J. 1993. "Don't worry, be happy: The postwar decline of private-sector unionism in the United States" in Jenson, J.; Mahon, R. (eds.) *The challenge of restructuring: North American labor movements respond* (Philadelphia, Temple University Press).

Sanyal, B. 1991. "Organizing the self-employed: The politics of urban informal sector" in *International Labour Review*, Vol. 130, No. 1, pp. 39–56, (Geneva, ILO).

Sherlock, S. 1996. "Class re-formation in Mumbai: Has organized labour risen to the challenge?" in *Economic and Political Weekly*, Review of Labour, pp. L 34-L38, December 28 (Bombay).

Song, Ho-Keun. 1999. *Labour unions in the Republic of Korea: Challenge and Choice*, Discussion Paper, Labour and Society Programme, International Institute for Labour Studies (Geneva, ILO).

Spalter-Roth, R. et al. 1994. "What do unions do for women?" in Sheldon Friedman et al (eds).; Restoring the Promise of American Labour Law, pp. 193–206 (Ithaca: ILR Press, Cornell University).

Tanzi, V.; Schuknecht, L. 1995. *The growth of government and the reform of the state in industrial countries*, IMF Working Paper, Fiscal Affairs Department (Washington).

Valkenburg, B. 1996. "Individualization and solidarity: The challenge of modernization" in Leisink, P. et al (eds). *The challenge of trade unions in Europe: Innovation or adaptation*, Cheltenham, Brookfield, Edward Elgar).

Webster, E.; Adler, G. 1998. *Towards a class compromise in South Africa's double transition: bargained liberalization and consolidation of democracy*, Paper presented at 14th World Congress of Sociology, Montreal, 26 July – 1 August.

Wong, E. 1999. *The partnership of trade unions in national development programmes and in the promotion of skill mobility among workers*, Paper presented at Regional Meeting on Organized Labour in the 21st Century, Seoul, 7–8 December.

NOTES

1   The ILO studies have been carried out in Brazil, Canada, Chile, Ghana, India, Israel, Japan, Republic of Korea, Lithuania, Niger, South Africa, Spain, Sweden, Tunisia, USA, and Zimbabwe. In preparing this overview paper, I have drawn on findings from the following studies: Japan (Inoue, 1999), Republic of Korea (Song, 1999), Israel (Nathanson et al., 1999), India (Bhattacherjee, 1999), Sweden (Fahlbeck, 1999), Lithuania (Dovideniene, 1999) and South Africa (Bezuidenhout, A. 1999).

2   This aspect is discussed in the ILO study on union responses to globalization in Japan (Inoue, 1999).

3   The union structures which evolved in the industrialized countries conform to two categories identified by Rogers (1993) namely: the high density centralized case (HDCC) and the low density decentralized case (LDDC). In both cases, unions gained ground in industries or enterprises, positioned at vantage points in the markets for products or services, and in the process gained significant outcomes for labour.

4   The term "labour aristocracy" derives from the privileges conferred on skilled workers drawn into urban areas on improved terms and conditions of employment. Their position as pioneers among the ranks of an economically powerful middle class enabled them to claim numerous rights and privileges in urban labour markets. They were politically important allies of the State, and in that capacity were entitled to a range of benefits which included higher wages, better working conditions, civic amenities and social security benefits.

5   The Histadrut in Israel is a case in point. The enactment of the National Health Insurance Law in 1994 severed the links between trade unions and the provision of health care. The emergence of competitive providers of heath care led to a 60 per cent fall in union membership (Nathanson et al., 1999). It follows that the provision of services is a necessary but not a sufficient condition for enhancing union membership. As much attention needs to be directed to the provision of services under competitive conditions.

6   According to Webster and Adler (1998) the pact was already breaking up. The debt crisis of the mid-1970s and the structural adjustment programmes of the Bretton Woods institutions had caused disenchantment among labour. The authors argue that the moral struggle against the violation of the

    pact fuelled many of the pro-democracy movements in the 1980s and the 1990s. The crisis of the development pact led to two distinct but connected projects: democratization to replace authoritarian political regimes; and economic restructuring to replace State protectionism.

7   Valkenburg (1996) argues that consequent to the rise of individualism, collective frames of reference are losing significance. These were based on an industrial class society, from which people derived part of their individual and social identity; and are losing significance.

8   This was noted earlier in the context of Israel. See Nathanson et al., 1999.

9   There has been a noticeable change in union attitudes towards work traditionally performed by women within the household. Among the industrialized countries, unions increasingly campaign for better community services for children and dependents; parental leave for working parents; training facilities for working women; and the increased representation of women in leadership positions within trade unions (Spalter-Roth et al., 1994). These concerns are just beginning to surface in union strategies in the developing world.

10 There are interesting precedents for union efforts to organize non-traditional members in the context of industrialized countries. For instance, in the United States the AFL-CIO has laid emphasis on organizing less skilled workers, women and minority groups in the service industries (Bronfenbrenner et al., 1998). There have also been innovative approaches to organizing low- skilled workers in small enterprises under the aegis of area-specific organizations. These initiatives might provide useful lessons for similar organizing efforts in developing countries.

11 In India, the real wages and non-wage benefits negotiated through company union structures increased during the 1980s. This happened mainly in capital-intensive industries which opted for technological upgrading. It also appears that certain regions of India which are late entrants to the field of industrialization have derived special benefits from the new bargaining structures. The new entrants have had a comparative advantage: they are better endowed with infrastructure, are pro-business, and they are less affected by militant unionism. These regions also claim a congenial environment for human resource management and non-antagonistic labour relations. These features in turn have significantly influenced the pace and pattern of industrial development in different regions of India. Employment and wages declined over the years in other parts of the country, where there were large labour intensive industries in the past and where militant unionism fiercely resisted new technology. Such industries became virtually extinct and the regions which harboured them became industrial wastelands. The textile mills of western India and the jute mills of eastern India are cases in point (Sherlock, 1996).

12 This point has been elaborated in relation to the observed increase in real wages of agricultural labourers in Kerala, India (Jose, 1994).

Steven Oates

8. INTERNATIONAL LABOUR STANDARDS: THE CHALLENGES OF THE 21st CENTURY

1. INTRODUCTION

The year 2000 is no doubt as good a time as any to reflect afresh on why the International Labour Organisation should have come into being in the 20th Century and why it should continue into the 21st. At the top of the list of answers to both questions is *international labour standards*.

It is not just nostalgia which might lead to a brief retrospective on 1919. Naturally, the humanitarian considerations in favour of more decent working lives, which had been becoming more and more difficult to ignore since the end of the previous century, provided an idealist as well as a practical orientation for a different kind of international organisation alongside the League of Nations. Of course, it was also the particular political environment in Europe around 1917 to 1919 which nurtured the insight that the labour movement – and, to maintain equilibrium, employer interests – could and should be embraced in policy-making and decision-taking at both international and national levels. But it was the creative genius behind the notion that a system of international standard-setting in the labour and social sphere could be the means of harnessing these social forces in order to serve those human objectives, while at the same time addressing the demands of *international trade* and thus economic development, which was to be the defining characteristic of the ILO.

All of this strikes similar chords in the year 2000 to those echoing from eighty years ago. Plainly, though, the aura of the past which is often perceived around international labour standards is not something which appeals much in the new era. So the main challenge now has to be to isolate the elements of the normative complex likely to prove most viable, relevant and adaptable to conditions in, say, the next eighty years or so.

2. SOCIAL DIALOGUE, TRIPARTISM AND CONSENSUS

The tripartite composition of the ILO remains crucial to the standard-setting function for at least three reasons. First, it is obvious that, when discussion is to centre on

R. Blanpain and C. Engels (eds), The ILO and the Social Challenge of the 21st Century, 93–103.
© 2001 *Kluwer Law International. Printed in Great Britain.*

conditions in the workplace, people with practical experience of the subject matter are the best equipped to know what the problems are and what might be the best ways of trying to address them. This is certainly the case as regards technical work processes (occupational safety and health, working time, etc.); but those workers and employers are also going to have the sort of realistic approach to more wide-ranging aspects of working life (such as wage and benefits systems, collective bargaining, employment and training systems) which must colour more general policy-making.

Secondly, it is as employers and workers that people have to function within the context of the prevailing labour standards. They are naturally going to do this more willingly and effectively – and the standards themselves are going to be implemented more satisfactorily – when it is they themselves who have taken part in the determination of their contents and they are not merely faced with a set of regulations imposed from above.

A third, slightly different, point is that a tripartite approach to all kinds of social and labour questions is one which seems to be rather more favourable to consensus-creation – and, arguably, implementation – than other modes of operation. The catalogue of international labour standards is full of examples of where the ILO's tripartite structure has facilitated progress: some of the early instruments adopted immediately after the First World War and in the 1920's are little short of epoch-making in the story of human rights development;[1] and the period after the Second World War was most fertile of all, with a succession of Conventions laying down concrete obligations on the foundation of the thinking behind the 1948 Universal Declaration of Human Rights.[2] This, then, is economic and social standard-setting with a strong civil and political flavour. In fact, the civil and political overtones of the Organisation's tripartite structure are so strong, that the whole concept of *social dialogue* eventually tends towards a qualitative change, in which the traditional social partners (employers' and workers' organisations) strive to increase their representativeness by reaching out to other non-governmental civil bodies and social organisms (which poses the ILO a challenge of a different order).

3. The Breadth of International Labour Standards

Assuming that an historical perspective is not necessarily the most attractive, perhaps one which takes in the very wide scope of the ILO's instruments will help. The fundamental "core" is now considered rather solid and complete, following the adoption of the two basic child labour Conventions.[3] In 1993, the Governing Body pinpointed four other Conventions[4] as priority ones on which frequent reporting was desirable, and it is easy to see why. Labour inspection is a key function of administration, since the whole body of labour legislation and regulations on all substantive matters depends on either good will and a law-abiding spirit in the workplace or effective enforcement mechanisms. Active employment policy should be the vehicle for promoting full, productive and freely-chosen employment: Convention No. 122 is the prime example of those instruments in the form of an international labour standard which create valuable obligations on the State but are essentially conceived in terms which establish a framework adaptable to countries at all stages of development.[5] And Convention No. 144 is another framework Convention (almost unique, by the way, in that it lays down no actual *labour* standards itself), providing this time for mechanisms appropriate to national conditions in each country, so as to ensure tripartite consultation on all international and national aspects of substantive labour standards.

Only slightly further afield, a larger group of Conventions (and perhaps a handful of Recommendations) emerge which elaborate on various other essential components of a *decent work*[6] régime. In the ILO of the year 2000, this concept would in any event merit at the very least a short digression. But in fact there is no diversion at all from the present theme of a viable and vital system of international labour standards. The idea of *decent work* takes on board the overwhelming fact of economic globalisation – with the transformation of the nature of enterprises, not least by dint of new information technologies and the now almost universal acceptance of market forces as a determinant. It then balances it with a changing social consciousness, in which social division and exclusion are perceived as both unjust and counter-productive. Its singularity is, in the right hands, its capacity to identify both the components of a tolerable and sustainable working life and the means of securing it. By its focus on the four-fold strategic objective of promotion of rights at work, employment, social protection and social dialogue, it sets the scene for concerted action on all the elements of work which can be said to be decent.

The Conventions which assist in this task will thus include ones dealing with the more general responsibilities of a labour administration,[7] particularly that of extending its functions into more informal types of employment where a regulatory culture does not operate. The main Conventions[8] and Recommendations[9] describing in greater detail how employment policies can be formulated and implemented will also appear. Then there will be a judicious representation of the leading Conventions on social policy,[10] wages,[11] occupational safety and health,[12] working time,[13] home work,[14] labour clauses in public contracts,[15] occupational health services,[16] prevention of major industrial accidents,[17] migrant workers,[18] indigenous and tribal peoples,[19] seafarers.[20] The income aspect of social protection is at present undergoing fresh examination in the ILO, but in any comprehensive view of *decent work* reference can certainly be made to some basic standards here too.[21]

There can be more, of course. But one fact which must be put over more effectively is that the catalogue of international labour standards contains instruments of several different kinds. Some Conventions enshrine *principles and rights* regarded as fundamental; some describe social and labour *policies* together with modes of operation, structures and procedures for implementing them; some suggest precise *regulations* to deal with workplace problems; some combine these elements. What is not correct is to suppose that all labour standards are about regulations in the work place, with the implication that "labour standards" necessarily raise labour costs and lead to loss of

95

competitiveness. Many of the above – relating, for example, to employment policy or occupational safety and health – will, on the contrary, tend to have rather favourable consequences for enterprises in terms of, among other things, productivity. Nor is it too much to argue that international labour standards in general contribute to sustainable development.

4. RATIFICATIONS

At the same time, it should be obvious that, when the whole list of (as at 1 July 2000) 183 Conventions and 4 Protocols – with in all 6,763 ratifications[22] – and 191 Recommendations looms on the horizon, there is a crying need for simplification. One approach to this is a sort of constitutional housekeeping involving the *withdrawal* of obsolete Recommendations and Conventions which can never come into force, and the *abrogation* of certain other obsolete Conventions.[23] A simple and immediate way of simplifying, though, is to make the whole scenario less "busy", by ceasing references to unhelpful non-disaggregated statistics, and selecting instead the instruments which lay down real obligations for States or give guidance which is actually relevant and useful.

Steps have been taken in this direction since 1979,[24] when the first distinctions were drawn by the Governing Body of the ILO between Conventions regarded as ones to be promoted on a priority basis and other Conventions. The latest stage in this process, which was resumed in a slightly different form in 1995 by a Working Party of the ILO Governing Body on Policy regarding the Revision of Standards, has enabled the identification of some 68 Conventions, 3 Protocols and 60 Recommendations considered to be "up-to-date".[25] ILO publications and compilations have of course long featured the instruments regarded as most relevant. But the large numbers of ratifications held out as significant have not yet been purged of all of the ones which do not carry any actual substantive obligations (in particular, Conventions not in force either at all or for given countries, and Conventions which only bring formal revision of final Articles concerning matters such as requirements for coming into force). Doing that in a way which analyses the meaningful obligations on States would give a more comprehensible and clearer image of each country's and the world's real commitment to international labour standards.

Is there, then, a further problem in a weakened willingness among member States to ratify ILO Conventions? Although it is certainly possible to point to lower numbers of ratifications of many of the more recent Conventions, ratifications of the fundamental and several other Conventions have in the last five years increased rather impressively.[26] It cannot, moreover, be assumed that absence of ratification means a Convention is necessarily given no effect. Besides, there is an inescapable mathematical logic in diminishing numbers of new ratifications of older Conventions: the more ratifications of, say, Convention No. 87 are registered, the fewer remain to be registered – so that a rate of something like 10 per year can surely not be sustained for long (especially since it is clearly the countries with the most serious difficulties which will take longest to reach that stage). In this case, a slower rate of ratification is really a sign that qualitative as well as quantitative progress has been made. This is a point which has perhaps not been put across too well.

Ratification matters because it creates a legal obligation on the State. Therein lies no doubt one of several interesting challenges for a normative organisation such as the ILO, in the sense that the creation of international legal norms which bind States ought to be a concern not only of the ILO and the States in question but – in different ways – of other actors in the multilateral system. In particular, it is sometimes striking that some international organisations, such as financial institutions, may not have regarded the fact that a given State is bound by the obligations of a given international labour Convention as any constraint on new advice or obligations with which they face a State. One example might be where a developing country bound by Convention No. 81 to ensure the operations of a labour inspection system is placed in the impossible position of obtaining monetary or financial help only on the condition that it reduces government spending on labour inspection and fails to discharge its obligations under that Convention. In a multilateral system where the rule of international and national law, as well as the indispensable role of social and labour standards in the achievement of sustainable development and even short-term competitiveness, is to be given greater weight, there may be an argument here which could perhaps be put more strongly.

5. THE DECLARATION ON FUNDAMENTAL PRINCIPLES AND RIGHTS AT WORK

In any event, perception in this area came in the 1990s to fix on a failure of the ILO to respond to contemporary needs. Specifically, not all (the most important) Conventions had been ratified by all (the most important) States, which were therefore not held to account for themselves when failures of implementation occurred. More generally, international debate in the context of economic globalisation – notably at the 1995 World Summit for Social Development in Copenhagen – re-focused attention on basic workers' rights and the centrality of the goal of full, productive and freely-chosen employment; and – notably by way of the 1996 Ministerial Conference of the World Trade Organisation in Singapore – on the role of the ILO in relation to labour standards. The Declaration adopted by the International Labour Conference in 1998 was the ILO's response.

The principles and rights identified by the Declaration are those dealt with in the fundamental Conventions on (a) freedom of association and collective bargaining; (b) forced or compulsory labour; (c) child labour; and (d) discrimination in employment and occupation.[27] The way forward reaffirmed by the Declaration is, first, advisory services and technical cooperation in order to promote ratification and implementation of the fundamental Conventions; and, second, assistance in promoting the principles even in the absence of ratification. This, then, constitutes an ILO contribution to strategy for creating a climate propitious to economic and social development. The key tools in this strategy are indicated in the Follow-Up which forms an integral part of the Declaration: regular reporting under article 19(5)(e) of the ILO Constitution on unratified fundamental Conventions leads to examination by a specially created group of experts and then the Governing Body;[28] and a global report by the Director-General each year on one of the four categories of fundamental principles and rights leads to a discussion at the Conference.[29]

For the present purpose, the Declaration process can perhaps be seen as both a stimulant and a manifestation of a process long-since engrained in the ILO *Weltanschauung*, but clearly in need of restatement. That is precisely the process which consists of deciding at the international level what are the common standards, principles and rights which should operate throughout the world; of pinpointing obstacles in the way of applying them at the national level; and of doing practical things to overcome those obstacles. Certainly the Declaration brings new advantages of higher visibility, greater universality and improved potential for practical action. At the same time, it is sometimes useful to emphasise the continuity of this process. With the partial exception of Convention No. 138, the fundamental Conventions had already obtained high rates of ratification before 1995, and the campaign for universal ratification of them launched by the Director-General of the ILO in May 1995 had already provoked a very good level of new ratifications. The idea of regular government reporting on implementation, plus consideration by an independent expert body as well as the tripartite International Labour Conference, is over 75 years old and has continued to produce palpable results. And the notion that technical cooperation should draw on the provisions of international labour standards and should be used to help member States fulfil standards-related obligations had already been gaining currency. The process of which the Declaration is a part, then, logically flows back into the broader stream of normative action as a means of promoting economic and social development; and the question is again how the *modus operandi* of international labour standards responds. So, there are more ratifications of fundamental Conventions: what consequences does this bring?

6. SUPERVISION

The ILO's supervisory procedures amount to one of the best guarantees you can have that international labour standards will be applied.[30] In their essence they are not complicated. Member States of the ILO have an obligation under article 22 of the Constitution to supply regular information on the legal and other measures taken to meet the requirements of the Conventions they have ratified. The Constitution recognised in 1919 that voluntary ratification should be a necessary step between the adoption of Conventions by the Conference and the coming into force of the State's obligation to implement them; and this is one of the timeless facts of life which dictated the approach to the Declaration taken by the Conference in 1998. The government reports containing that information are examined by the Committee of Experts on the Application of Conventions and Recommendations, which functions on principles of independence, impartiality and objectivity and, wherever there are problems of implementation, addresses comments to the governments concerned.[31] The main part of this objective analysis is subsequently examined by the tripartite Conference Committee on the Application of Standards,[32] at which government representatives in the most serious cases are invited to answer the criticisms made. This procedure has since 1964 contributed to 2,230[33] cases where satisfaction has been attained in respect of problems raised, as well as many other uncounted positive developments. The regular supervisory procedure is supplemented by special complaints procedures. The article 19 procedure for reporting on unratified Conventions is used each year for different (non-fundamental) Conventions and applies to Recommendations too.[34]

Several factors contribute to the success of this system. The main one is the happy combination of impartial expert review followed by tripartite discussion of difficulties. The former depends on dedicated and sustained servicing of the Committee of Experts, which involves active, comparative legal expertise and the capacity to conduct dialogue with the States concerned through informal channels as well as the formal supervisory exchanges. The latter invokes the social and more political arguments and pressures which may be necessary in order to help bring about the legal (and more political) changes within a State which will in turn lead to recognition of the problem of application and the taking of concrete measures to deal with it. Employers' and workers' organisations are a vital part of this, both through their participation in the Conference and through exercise of their less well-known power to make observations on problems of application for the consideration of the Committee of Experts. So far so good. Now for the complications.

The 1919 Constitution provided for annual reporting on all ratified Conventions. When total ratifications are into the thousands, this is clearly neither feasible nor desirable. Governing Body decisions over recent decades – to space out article 22 reports first every two years then every five except for Conventions such as the fundamental and priority ones where reporting remains two-yearly but may be more frequent if the Committee of Experts so considers or where reports are already overdue or have not replied to previous requests for information – have thus had the very regrettable consequence of making the reporting system complex to the point where it borders on the arcane. This is in itself a serious shortcoming in a system which has to be transparent, understandable and attractive to all concerned if it is to serve its purpose to the full. In addition, it means that the system constantly risks failure to pick up in adequate time significant problems of application of non-priority Conventions (including ones referred to in paragraph 9, above, which help define the notion of *decent work*) where reporting is normally only five-yearly. Thus, in the third place, the volume of undifferentiated reporting and analytical work resting on the shoulders of government administrations and national employers' and workers' organisations as well as the International Labour Office and the supervisory bodies may cause severe difficulties in dealing even with fundamental Conventions.

The developments which culminated in the adoption of the Declaration in 1998 hold other lessons too. One is the confirmation that there is still a strong consensus around the need for normative action *including supervision*[35] in the social and labour sphere. Another – which should surprise no-one – is that constituents and administrations of all kinds require greater focus and prioritisation in such normative action. A third – which may be the greatest task of all before the Office in terms of strategy, programming, implementation of objectives and operationalisation of the concept of *decent work* – is that priorities and plans of action for technical cooperation should be determined by reference to both fundamental principles and rights at work and, more widely, embrace respect for and aim to promote international labour standards.[36]

The moral of this story seems to be that the supervisory processes should focus themselves more. It would no doubt be putting it too crudely to say that they should concern themselves only with a select group of Conventions relating to fundamental principles and rights and a *decent work* régime. However, there are, equally, clear arguments for a greater *give-and-take* vis-à-vis international labour standards: *giving* guidance on precepts by which decisions on technical cooperation and advisory services should be offered by the Office – *taking* into consideration the prevailing feelings of constituents as to the real priorities; *giving* information to constituents and the field structure on the difficulties of implementing standards – *taking* notice of how the practical problems arise and progress which is achieved in terms of the knowledge/service/advocacy trilogy of the ILO's modes of action.

One way of refocusing might be for the supervisory bodies to adopt a more "country-centred" methodology. This would imply some presentational changes, an endeavour to put to the member States a more coherent and cogent statement of the problems of application in a way which each State can more readily assimilate. It would have to derive, furthermore, from a greater *give-and-take* between the Office's work in servicing the supervisory bodies on the one hand and its technical cooperation and advisory work relating to employment, social protection and social dialogue on the other.

A suitable occasion for this kind of reorientation might be the review of the article 22 reporting system expected in 2001. The current periodicity of reporting on ratified Conventions (basically, two-yearly or five-yearly, but with various exceptions) was decided in November 1993[37] and came into operation in 1996 for a trial five-year cycle. It has unfortunately not yet produced any appreciable rise in the percentages of reports actually received,[38] while States' new commitments, especially to the fundamental Conventions, have nevertheless continued to increase. The national administrative burden of reporting is a significant one not only for developing countries, while the capacity of the Office to discharge the tasks associated with servicing the supervisory bodies is sorely stretched. A move towards a radical simplification of the reporting system could be very welcome, then: a system where each government would owe just one report each year but that report would include all *necessary* information on problems arising under *all* ratified Conventions is quite conceivable.

This kind of approach might in fact be found to enhance the credibility and widespread respect persistently accorded both within member States and among other international organisations to the ILO's supervisory mechanisms, with their prudent mix of independent expert review, tripartite dialogue and special complaints procedures. It may be that, in a "country-centred" rather than a "Convention-centred" perspective – that is, one which tries to see the problems of application more from the point of view of the member State and its constituents as well as from that of the international organisation – the supervisory system finds it somewhat easier to prioritise, to concentrate on the most important issues, while making itself less esoteric and more accessible.

7. New Kinds of International Labour Standards?

The approach in all of the above is to try and build a bridge away from the international standard-setting born of an industrialising world and struggling for relevance to countries at all stages of economic, social and political development towards a normative construct which will survive in a new century characterised more by economic globalisation and a rather different international architecture. One way in which the ILO is perhaps succeeding in adapting itself is by re-designing its mid- to long-term objectives and looking anew at the tools it might use to achieve them.[39] Given their history, international labour standards remain the object of a shared commitment among the ILO's constituents, although there is now an undoubted perception that they should have a qualitatively greater visibility, effectiveness and relevance.[40] This leads to exploration of new means by which they might be translated into real changes in the workplace,[41] and debates as to the form as well as the content of future instruments which might be adopted in the ILO. The evolution of this subject has not yet ceased.

Notes

1 E.g., the first child labour Convention – Minimum Age (Industry), 1919 (No. 5) – or the Forced Labour Convention, 1930 (No. 29).

2 E.g., the Freedom of Association and Protection of the Right to Organise Convention, 1948 (No. 87), and the Right to Organise and Collective Bargaining Convention, 1949 (No. 98). Not far behind these came the Equal Remuneration Convention, 1951 (No. 100), the Abolition of Forced Labour Convention, 1957 (No. 105), and the Discrimination (Employment and Occupation) Convention, 1958 (No. 111).

3 Minimum Age Convention, 1973 (No. 138), and Worst Forms of Child Labour Convention, 1999 (No. 182).

4 Labour Inspection Convention, 1948 (No. 81); Labour Inspection (Agriculture), 1969 (No. 129); Employment Policy, 1964 (No. 122); and Tripartite Consultation (International Labour Standards), 1976 (No. 144).

5 Convention No. 122 is also one of an interesting few which provide for dialogue (consultations) outside the employer and worker sphere – in this case, with "persons affected" by the policies and measures in question. See Article 3 of the Convention.

6 For the general introduction to this concept, see Decent Work, Report of the Director-General, International Labour Conference, 87th Session, Geneva,1999.

7 Labour Administration Convention, 1978 (No. 150): see especially Article 7. See also Labour Statistics Convention, 1985 (No. 160).

8   Employment Service Convention, 1948 (No. 88); Human Resources Development Convention, 1975 (No. 142); Private Employment Agencies Convention, 1997 (No. 181); Termination of Employment Convention, 1982 (No. 158); Vocational Rehabilitation and Employment (Disabled Persons) Convention, 1983 (No. 159).

9   Employment Policy Recommendation, 1964 (No. 122); Employment Policy (Supplementary Provisions) Recommendation, 1984 (No. 169); Job-Creation in Small and Medium-Sized Enterprises Recommendation, 1998 (No. 189).

10 Social Policy (Basic Aims and Standards) Convention, 1962 (No. 117).

11 Minimum Wage Fixing Convention, 1970 (No. 131); Protection of Wages Convention, 1949 (No. 95).

12 Working Environment (Air Pollution, Noise and Vibration) Convention, 1977 (No. 148); Occupational Safety and Health Convention, 1981 (No. 155); Chemicals Convention, 1990 (No. 170).

13 Weekly Rest (Industry) Convention, 1921 (No, 14); Weekly Rest (Commerce and Offices) Convention, 1957 (No. 106); Holidays with Pay Convention (Revised), 1970 (No. 132); Paid Educational Leave Convention, 1974 (No. 140); Part-Time Work Convention, 1994 (No. 175). See also Reduction of Hours of Work Recommendation, 1962 (No. 116).

14 Home Work Convention, 1996 (No. 177).

15 Labour Clauses (Public Contracts), 1949 (No. 94).

16 Occupational Health Services Convention, 1985 (No. 161).

17 Prevention of Major Industrial Accidents Convention, 1993 (No. 174).

18 Migration for Employment Convention (Revised), 1949 (No. 97); Migrant Workers (Supplementary Provisions) Convention, 1975 (No. 143).

19 Indigenous and Tribal Peoples Convention, 1989 (No. 169).

20 Merchant Shipping (Minimum Standards) Convention, 1976 (No. 147).

21 See the Social Security (Minimum Standards) Convention, 1952 (No. 102); the Employment Promotion and Protection against Unemployment Convention, 1988 (No. 168); and now the Maternity Protection Convention, 2000 (No. 183).

22 See Report III (Part 2), International Labour Conference, 88th Session, 2000.

23 *Abrogation* of Conventions which are in force was the object of the Instrument for the Amendment of the Constitution of the International Labour Organisation which was adopted by the 85th Session of the Conference in 1997 but which, for want of ratifications, is not yet in force. The first *withdrawals* of obsolete Conventions took place at the 88th Session in 2000, in respect of five Conventions adopted in the 1930's which never came into force. The possible withdrawal of 20 obsolete Recommendations is on the agenda of the 89th (2001) Session.

24 See Final Report of the Working Party on International Labour Standards, ILO Official Bulletin Vol. LXII, 1979 (Series A). This was reviewed 8 years later: Report of the Working Party on International Labour Standards, ILO Official Bulletin, Vol.LXX, 1987 (Series A).

25 GB.277/LILS/WP/PRS/1/1 provides a detailed summary of the situation as of March 2000. Convention No. 183 and Recommendation No. 191 concerning maternity protection can now be added to the list of up-to-date instruments. The count here is not the same as that described in paras. 7 to 10 above in relation to *decent work*, because there the starting point is the "core" Conventions and the movement is outwards: contrariwise, the Working Party starts from the totality and moves inwards. Furthermore, the 68 + 1 do not include several Conventions which are in force and which create meaningful obligations on States, but which have been revised by more recent Conventions on the same subject – the latter being, Q.E.D., more "up-to-date".

26 See GB 277/LILS/5 (March 2000), which indicated a total of 167 new ratifications of the seven fundamental Conventions in that period. As of July 2000, the total is nearer 180, in addition to 30 ratifications of Convention No. 182 – a record for the first year of any Convention.

27 That is to say, Conventions Nos. 87 and 98; 29 and 105; 138; and 100 and 111. As regards child labour, Convention No.182 has since been recognised as belonging to this list.

28 See Review of annual reports under the Follow-Up to the ILO Declaration on Fundamental Principles and Rights at Work: Part I (Introduction by the ILO Declaration Expert-Advisers to the compilation

of annual reports, Geneva, March 2000) in GB.277/3/1; and Part II (Compilation of annual reports by the International Labour Office) in GB.277/3/2.

29 See Your Voice at Work (Global report under the Follow-Up to the ILO Declaration on Fundamental Principles and Rights at Work), International Labour Conference, 88th Session, 2000, Report I(B).

30 See in general Handbook of procedures relating to international labour Conventions and Recommendations, International Labour Office, Geneva, Rev.2/1998.

31 The most recent report is in Report III (Part 1A), International Labour Conference, 88th Session, 2000.

32 See Report of the Committee on the Application of Standards, International Labour Conference, 88th Session, Geneva, 2000, Provisional Record 23 (Parts One and Two).

33 See footnote 31, para. 100.

34 See footnote 31: the Committee of Experts makes a separate General Survey of the subject concerned, which appears as Part 1B of its report. The most recent General Survey was on tripartite consultation.

35 The terms "normative" and "supervisory" are of course not entirely apt in the context of the Declaration. But the recognition of obligations, principles and rights contained in the body of the Declaration and the follow-up devices contained in its Annex are arguably at least analogous to normative and supervisory process.

36 See Annex to the Declaration, Part III.B.2; and Resolution concerning the role of the ILO in technical cooperation (Conclusions, Para. 4), adopted in 1999 by the 87th Session of the Conference.

37 GB.258/6/19.

38 Following highs of over 80 registered into the 1980's, the percentage of reports received in time for the session of the Committee of Experts was 61.4 in November 1999, compared with 63.3 in 1996, although there are some signs of the fall bottoming out: see footnote 32 above, Part Two, statistical table D (page 23/124). Still, reporting performances continue to stand up well to comparison with figures for human rights instruments in other international organisations.

39 See, e.g., Decent Work (footnote 6 above); and GB.276/PFA/9 (November 1999): Programme and Budget Proposals for 2000–01: Approval of the detailed budget and further development of strategic budgeting.

40 Reply by the Director-General to the discussion of his Report, International Labour Conference, 88th Session, Geneva, 2000, Provisional Record 25.

41 The desire for non-legislative means is one reason for the renewed emphasis on collective bargaining as a way of fixing working conditions; but other voluntary means might also be sought.

Anne Trebilcock

9. THE ILO DECLARATION ON FUNDAMENTAL PRINCIPLES AND RIGHTS AT WORK: A NEW TOOL

1. INTRODUCTION

With the adoption of the ILO Declaration on Fundamental Principles and Rights at Work in 1998, the world community renewed a commitment to promote universal respect of these core values and reached consensus on their definition. The Declaration also reaffirmed the ILO's responsibilities to its Member States. This mutual pledge represents part of a broader consensus about emerging rules for the global economy. The promotional Follow-up that accompanies the Declaration *encourages* countries' efforts to respect these principles and rights at to work. Under the Follow-up, regularly updated information on efforts made by countries not yet having ratified the eight fundamental ILO Conventions is produced to complement what is already available in the context of established supervisory procedures for ratified Conventions. Under the Declaration, the roles of ILO advisory services and technical cooperation, as well as of employers' and workers' organisations, are of heightened importance. Steadfast political will of governments and sufficient resources to sustain their progress on fundamental principles and rights at work are key elements for the Declaration Follow-up to succeed. The paper looks at the main features of the Declaration, its impact so far both within and outside the ILO, its origins, and its potential as a tool for development.

2. WHAT IS THE ILO DECLARATION ON FUNDAMENTAL PRINCIPLES AND RIGHTS AT WORK?

Adopted on 17 June 1998, the ILO Declaration on Fundamental Principles and Rights at Work represents a mutual commitment between the ILO and its Member States, based on existing ILO constitutional obligations. The Declaration begins by recalling the endorsement of the principles and rights set out in the ILO Constitution, together with the undertaking by countries to "work towards attaining the overall objectives of the Organisation to the best of their resources and fully in line with their

R. Blanpain and C. Engels (eds), The ILO and the Social Challenge of the 21st Century, 105–116.
© 2001 *Kluwer Law International. Printed in Great Britain.*

specific circumstances".[1] After recalling the existence of Conventions recognised as fundamental both inside and outside the Organisation,[2] the Declaration sets out the obligations of the Member States and of the Organisation.

Under the Declaration, all 175 of the ILO's member States "have an obligation, arising from the very fact of membership in the Organisation, to respect, promote and realise, in good faith and in accordance with the Constitution",[3] these four categories of fundamental principles and rights at work:

- freedom of association and the effective recognition of the right to collective bargaining,
- elimination of forced or compulsory labour,
- effective abolition of child labour and
- elimination of discrimination in employment or occupation.

The significance of the ILO Declaration lies in the universal reach of these fundamental principles and rights even to countries that have not yet ratified the relevant ILO Conventions[4] and the coupling of a reporting mechanism with offers of assistance to Governments. ILO member States have thus acknowledged their obligation to respect, realise and promote the rights and principles in the Declaration, whether this be done through ratification and implementation of the core ILO Conventions or otherwise.

At the same time, the Declaration places an obligation on the ILO itself to make full use of its "constitutional, operational and budgetary resources", to mobilise external resources and support, and to encourage other international organisations with which the ILO has established relations to support these efforts.[5] Thus technical cooperation and advisory services are to be offered to:

- promote ratification and implementation of the fundamental Conventions,
- assist all member States, whether they have ratified those treaties or not, to respect, promote and realise the principles in the Declaration and/or their obligations under ratified Conventions, and
- help member states in their efforts to create a climate for economic and social development.[6]

Operationally, the Declaration means that countries displaying the political will to achieve enhanced respect for the fundamental principles and rights at work deserve stepped-up support for their efforts.

A promotional Follow-up to the Declaration, described *infra*, is established by paragraph 4 of the Declaration. Its final paragraph (para. 5) stresses that "labour standards should not be used for protectionist trade purposes", and that neither the Declaration nor its Follow-up shall be invoked or otherwise used for such purposes or in any way call into question a country's comparative advantage.[7]

In contrast to the 183 Conventions, 191 Recommendations and numerous resolutions adopted over the years by the International Labour Conference, the new ILO instrument's designation as a "solemn declaration" sets it apart as a rare species in ILO usage.[8] Consistent with UN practice, a declaration is a "formal and solemn instrument suitable for rare occasions when principles of lasting importance are being enunciated".[9] The principles and rights in the Declaration are just that: they go to the essence of human dignity at work, touching upon bedrock values of freedom and equality.

3. A MEANINGFUL AND PROMOTIONAL FOLLOW-UP

But what is to prevent this lofty declaration from being forgotten soon after its adoption? The ILO Declaration is accompanied by a promotional Follow-up.[10] The Follow-up embraces a means of tracking and encouraging progress in respecting the fundamental principles and rights at work by countries in all regions. The devices for this are the annual review and the global reports, the setting of priorities for technical cooperation to support countries' efforts, and its implementation in practice. In each of these, there are roles for governments, employers' and workers' organisations and the ILO itself. The Declaration and its Follow-up are based on existing constitutional provisions.[11]

The first leg of the Follow-up involves annual reporting by countries that have not yet ratified all of the eight core ILO Conventions on these four subjects (the **annual review**, undertaken using report forms approved by the ILO Governing Body).[12] The purpose of the annual review is to provide an opportunity to review "the efforts made in accordance with the Declaration by Members which have not yet ratified all the fundamental Conventions".[13] The idea is to have each country establish its own baseline against which changes can be measured, and it is foreseen that countries will thereafter report on changes in law and practice.[14] In accordance with practice under article 23 of the ILO Constitution, the most representative organisations of employers and workers in a country are entitled to receive copies of their governments' reports. They as well as regional or international federations may make comments on the efforts being made by member States under the Declarartion. The International Labour Office produces a compilation of these annual reports, and of comments that are not in the nature of complaints. A group of seven independent ILO Declaration Expert-Advisers reviews this material during an annual five-day meeting and draws attention to any aspects that might call for a more in-depth discussion by the Governing Body.[15]

The second leg of the Follow-up is a review of the situation world wide ("a dynamic global picture") on one of these categories of principles and rights in turn, based on official sources (the **global report**). The global report is to serve as a basis for assessing the effectiveness of the assistance provided by the ILO and for determining priorities for the following period in the form of technical cooperation action plans.[16] The initial global report, on freedom of association and effective recognition of the right to collective bargaining, was the subject of heated debate at the International Labour Conference in June 2000.[17] It pointed out the contribution that freedom of association and collective bargaining – values long promoted by the ILO – can make to more participatory, transparent societies, which in turn promote economic growth and stability over time. After reviewing the main ways in which freedom of association and effective recognition of the right to collective bargaining remain to be meaningfully realised in many countries around the globe, the global report examined the effectiveness of ILO activities to promote them. It also suggested some possible points of concentration for the ILO's future work, and highlighted important important gaps in representation.

The discussion that took place on the global report is to serve as the basis for the third leg of the Follow-up: the setting of **priorities and action plans for technical cooperation** by the ILO Governing Body. This will take place for the first time in November 2000.[18] The next global reports will be on the elimination of all forms of forced or compulsory labour (2001), the effective abolition of child labour (2002) and the elimination of discrimination in respect of employment and occupation (2003), before the four-year cycle recommences. Each will lead to action plans to be adopted by the ILO Governing Body in relation to the category of principles and rights addressed by the respective global report.

The annual review, the global report and the technical cooperation priorities are interlinked. With roles for employers' and workers' organisations in relation to the drawing up of annual reports, in the discussion of the global report at the tripartite International Labour Conference, and in the determination of the priorities for technical cooperation in the tripartite ILO Governing Body, lively debate is a given in relation to the Declaration. The three-pronged Follow-up under the Declaration is designed to complement – and not to duplicate or interfere with – the long-standing supervisory procedures relating to ratified ILO Conventions and freedom of association principles.[19]

4. EXPERIENCE TO DATE UNDER THE FOLLOW-UP

What is new about the Follow-up? First of all, it is characterised as a promotional tool, to distinguish it from supervisory functions for ratified ILO Conventions. Its emphasis is on the positive and on encouraging improvements. The ILO is urging Member States to use the reporting obligation as an opportunity to look at where they stand, to identify possible obstacles to achieving full respect for the fundamental principles and rights, and to think through what action might be taken by themselves, with support from the ILO and other institutions, to improve the situation. At the same time, the Follow-up provides an important new information source about ILO constituents' views about the efforts being made by Member States to respect fundamental principles and rights at work. Furthermore, transparency of the process is ensured by reproduction of the compilation of reports in full for the ILO Governing

Body and on the public ILO website. The ILO Expert-Advisers have proposed revising the report forms to incorporate gender more explicitly as one means of eliciting fuller information on the social and economic conditions that influence respect for the principles and rights in the Declaration.

The initial (1999–2000) annual review under the Declaration Follow-up produced encouraging, if somewhat mixed, results. First of all the rate of reporting: overall it was 55.7 percent, which was acceptable for a first exercise but clearly left considerable room for improvement. A number of countries have used reporting as an opportunity to examine their own situations and to identify areas in which technical cooperation from the ILO or other sources might help overcome obstacles they face. Some workers' and employers' organisations have exercised their right to comment on Government reports or more generally on the efforts made; a few were involved in tripartite consultations on the drafting of the report. The ILO Governing Body endorsed the Expert-Advisers' recommendations that such organisations should be urged to participate more actively to use the Declaration in the promotional spirit in which it is intended (since it is not a complaints procedure).

As the group of ILO Declaration Expert-Advisers stressed in its first report, "The follow-up process under the Declaration charts the way for social progress. The promotional nature of the Follow-up is its distinctive feature. It operates by helping countries take stock of their situation and encouraging their real efforts through technical cooperation and other means. It reaches out to countries not yet engaged fully in the new process".[20]

5. Initial Impact of the Declaration and its Follow-up

It is still very early days to assess the impact of an instrument adopted only two years ago. Yet some effects are already clear. The Declaration has, first of all, helped the ILO bring greater focus its own activities, by serving as an axis around which much of its other work can be aligned. Since the Declaration involves a mutually reinforcing package of principles and rights that have been characterised as "enabling" – partly because they lay a foundation for the exercise of other rights – it fits nicely with interdisciplinary approaches to problem-solving and greater emphasis on development now found in the ILO's work programme.

Secondly, the Declaration and its Follow-up have stimulated many non-ratifying States to take a fresh look at the fundamental ILO Conventions. In a good number of cases, it has led to their ratification or to concrete steps in that direction. No longer is it seen as utopian to strive for nearly universal ratification of these basic instruments. For instance, the new Worst Forms of Child Labour Convention, 1999 (No. 182), has recorded more ratifications than any other ILO Convention in a comparable period.[21]

Thirdly, the Declaration and the principles and rights enshrined in it have enjoyed resonance in the international community. References have appeared in several other multilateral settings, most recently in the newly revised OECD Guidelines for

Multinational Enterprises. The multilateral consensus on trade and labour issues that emerged out of Copenhagen, Singapore and Geneva (see *infra*) remains intact following the events at the Seattle Ministerial Meeting in December 1999, and was reiterated at the UNCTAD X Conference in Bangkok in February 2000.

Fourthly, technical cooperation needs identified in relation to the Declaration have sparked considerable interest in the donor community (as at 1 September 2000, around US$45,000,000 had been given or pledged for use under the Declaration umbrella over the next three years). Thus a golden opportunity exists to demonstrate how technical cooperation can support improved respect for fundamental principles and rights at work, and how such respect can underpin sound, gender-sensitive development.

While the ILO Declaration is directed towards national governments and international organisations (and especially the ILO itself), it would be remiss to overlook the activities of private actors in relation to pursuing respect for core labour standards. In its outreach to private business, the United Nations last year established the Global Compact, which highlights a set of principles that multinational and other corporations are pledging to respect. Four of the nine principles in the Global Compact are the principles and rights contained in the ILO Declaration on Fundamental Principles and Rights at Work (the others address environmental issues). The Global Compact has enjoyed the support of both the ILO employer and trade union constituents, which have also undertaken a number of initiatives of their own to promote the ILO Declaration.

The events surrounding the World Trade Organisation Ministerial Meeting in Seattle in late 1999 tend to obscure the consensus that has already arisen around international labour standards and how they relate to development.[22] This consensus consists of four elements: (1) a renewed pledge for all countries to respect, realise and promote universal fundamental principles and rights at work as defined within the ILO, (2) an affirmation that labour standards may not be used for protectionist trade purposes, (3) reassurance that countries which play by the rules (labour and trade) deserve increased support for their efforts to make good on commitments they have undertaken, and (4) recognition that trade and labour standards are only part of a more complex equation involving many factors, ranging from investment policy to educational infrastructure. The ILO Declaration and the success of its Follow-up are key elements in this consensus.

Once a solid body of experience has been gained under the Follow-up, the International Labour Conference may wish to exercise a prerogative spelled out in the Declaration, i.e. to review the operation of the Follow-up to see whether it has adequately fulfilled its overall purpose.[23] A tentative balance sheet would suggest that while not perfect, the Declaration and its Follow-up are stimulating progress in a helpful way in many parts of the world.

6. WHAT WERE THE ORIGINS OF THE DECLARATION?

Part of the potential success of the Declaration and its Follow-up lie in its origins. The ideas taken up by the Declaration are rooted in the 1919 ILO Constitution and in particular in the universal values expressed in the 1944 Declaration of Philadelphia concerning the aims and purposes of the Organisation. Why, then, was a new Declaration adopted? Several reasons can be identified. First, the end of the 20th century was marked by increasing disquiet over the effects of globalisation and its effects on working people, related structural changes in the labour market that brought fresh challenges to established systems of individual and collective labour relationships, and an explosion of both free markets and democratic regimes. While there was heightened recognition of the need for a social pillar in the global economy, considerable controversy surrounded the question of how to achieve it. Proposals for a so-called "social clause" to link liberalised trade with decent labour standards provoked deep suspicion among many ILO Member States, and often seemed to create more noise than results. Counter accusations of social dumping and protectionism were leading nowhere in the multilateral system.

An important first step in moving beyond this impasse was the International Labour Conference discussion of the report of the ILO Director-General on the occasion of the ILO's 75th anniversary in 1994. This then led in the same year to a working party being established in the ILO Governing Body on the social dimensions of the liberalisation of international trade (recently renamed the Working Party on the Social Dimensions of Globalisation), which has served as useful forum for informal debate among ILO constituents.

In the meantime, important developments were occurring outside the ILO. The 1995 World Summit on Social Development, held in Copenhagen, yielded a high-level political commitment to "promote respect for relevant ILO Conventions, including those on the prohibition of forced and child labour, freedom of association, the right to organise and bargaining collectively, and the principles of non-discrimination".[24] This prompted the ILO to launch a ratification campaign that since 1995 has witnessed a 25% increase in the number of Member States bound by these Conventions. Most of that increase has occurred since adoption of the Declaration, suggesting its additional catalytic effect.[25]

The ILO's "soft" approach was given another shot in the arm by the publication of a study by the Organisation for Economic Co-operation and Development (OECD) in 1996, allaying possible fears that application of two core labour standards (on freedom of association and collective bargaining) might impact negatively on the competitiveness of countries in the context of trade liberalisation.[26]

The significance of fundamental rights at work was further reflected in part of the Final Declaration adopted by Ministers attending the first Ministerial Conference of the World Trade Organisation in Singapore in December 1996. While stressing that the comparative advantage of countries, particularly low-wage developing countries, should in no way be called into question, the Governments renewed their "commitment to the observance of internationally recognised core labour standards" and recalled that the ILO was the competent body to set and deal with these standards.[27]

This threw the ball back into the ILO's court. The Director-General at the time, Michel Hansenne, proposed the idea of a declaration accompanied by a suitable follow-up mechanism. After 18 months of extensive discussion in various instances of the Governing Body, the International Labour Conference debated a draft text and adopted the Declaration and its Follow-up on a tripartite basis on 17 June 1998. Within the context of the ILO's weighted voting system, the Declaration was adopted with 273 votes in favour, no votes against and 43 abstentions (the abstentions were cast by delegates from 21 States).[28] Two points have been characterised as instrumental in winning approval for the Declaration: the assurance that no new legal obligations were being created, and the legal foundation for the follow-up in article 19(5)(e) of the ILO Constitution.[29]

7. THE DECLARATION APPROACH

When the newly-elected Director-General of the ILO (Juan Somavía of Chile) presented his first report to the International Labour Conference in 1999, he highlighted the ILO Declaration as serving as a "point of reference for the entire global community".[30] Since October 1999, a special programme to promote the Declaration has been engaging in advocacy, supporting the Follow-up through workshops and report preparation, developing technical cooperation proposals with constituents and initiating research. Working through its many technical and field units, the ILO's direct support to its tripartite constituents in relation to fundamental principles and rights at work ranges from short-term advisory services and seminars to longer-term externally funded technical cooperation projects. Projects under the aegis of the ILO's separate International Programme for the Elimination of Child Labour (IPEC), labour law reform initiatives, capacity building for employers' and workers' organisations as well as labour administrations, programmes to put in place effective institutions for social dialogue and dispute prevention/resolution, projects to improve the status of women in the labour market, and those to create microcredit schemes as an alternative to bonded labour, serve as prime illustrations. Meetings to promote the Declaration have stressed activating ILO constituents to identify the chief obstacles they perceive to the realisation of each category of fundamental principles and rights, define action they themselves could take to remedy the situation in the short-term, and pinpoint how technical cooperation or technical assistance could assist them in these efforts.

A more detailed example may perhaps best illustrate how the Declaration approach can operate at the country level. The move to democracy and economic equilibrium in Indonesia has gone hand in glove with efforts to respect core labour standards. Before the economic crisis, Indonesia came in for heavy criticism by the ILO supervisory bodies for limitations on freedom of association and collective bargaining. (Indonesia had ratified the Collective Bargaining and Right to Organise Convention (No. 98) in 1957 but had encountered substantial difficulties in applying it in the context of a trade union monopoly linked to the ruling party.) The ratification of the Freedom of Association and Protection of the Right to Organise Convention (No. 87) in June 1998, with encouragement from the International Monetary Fund, and an

ILO direct contacts mission in August of that year swung open the door to cooperation between Indonesia and the ILO on core labour standards.

A letter of intent signed by the ILO and the President of Indonesia helped launch a
nationwide sensitisation campaign to mobilise support for the ratification (in June
1999) and implementation of the remaining fundamental ILO Conventions.
Indonesia became the first country in Asia to have ratified all of the fundamental ILO
Conventions (it has since been joined in this by Cambodia). Full consultations also
began on tripartite drafting of new labour legislation to address the challenges of a
global economy; some of this legislation has been enacted and other pieces are still
being developed. Led by the Indonesians themselves, the transition process has also
created capacity among workers, employers and government officials to widely disseminate the message of the ILO core Conventions throughout the country.
Accompanying the transition in a sustained manner has been possible for the ILO
only thanks to considerable support from the donor community. The Indonesian
experience has highlighted the successful "Declaration model" of a show of political
will on the part of the Government, the active involvement of organisations of
employers, workers and civil society, technical advisory support from the ILO, and
financial backing from the donor community.[31] For countries not yet having ratified
all of the fundamental Conventions, the Declaration approach has involved encouraging active participation of employer and worker representatives in the reporting
system and using that system as an opportunity to promote social dialogue.

8. Integrating Respect for Fundamental Principles and Rights as Part of Development

In the spirit of the Declaration, the ILO is pursuing important indirect support for its
member States by encouraging other intergovernmental organisations, financial institutions and bilateral donors to incorporate social concerns when they engage in their
own activities. This reflects the conviction that sound social policy is part and parcel
of attacking poverty and achieving sustainable economic growth. For this reason, the
ILO approaches fundamental principles and rights at work as a basic tool for the
creation of decent work and equitable development in countries around the globe.
These are topics that deserve considerably greater attention from the research and
development communities. The increased interest in issues such as good governance
and "voice" mechanisms as means of avoiding economic and financial crises opens up
opportunities for deepening understanding about the linkages between respect for
fundamental principles and rights at work and sustaining equitable development.

The principles and rights in the ILO Declaration are means towards an end: sound
and equitable economic development to improve the lives of all men and women.
They are principles and rights that enable the flowering of human potential and the
building of vibrant social institutions that can aid in the eradication of poverty. As
human rights, they form part of the heritage of all humankind. As inputs to economic
growth, they keep trade liberalisation and indeed modern capitalism viable. Countries

Anne Trebilcock

that have eliminated forced labour and the worst forms of child labour and have made important inroads against discrimination in employment and occupation are thriving economically. Respect for freedom of association reinforces popular participation and buttresses democratic institutions. Systems of collective bargaining and social dialogue create space for negotiations that can address an uneven distribution of the gains from economic growth. Independent organisations of employers and of workers can push for more transparent and hence more efficient public policies enjoying broad support across the population. We need to know more about successful strategies for achieving these results in different cultural contexts.

9. Concluding Remarks

As a universal definition of and commitment to fundamental principles and rights at work, the ILO Declaration on Fundamental Principles and Rights at Work and its Follow-up provide a key policy component for development aimed at improving the lives of working women and men all over the globe. For the ILO Declaration to achieve its potential as a new tool for development, efforts will be needed from the local to the international level. This means first of all stimulating greater awareness of the many possibilities the ILO Declaration and its Follow-up offer. Further, it implies continuing support for countries' genuine efforts to make greater respect for fundamental principles and rights part of their gender-sensitive development strategies.

Bibliography

H. Kellerson, "The ILO Declaration of 1998 on Fundamental Principles and Rights: A Challenge for the Future", *International Labour Review*, Geneva, 1998, Vol. 137, No. 2, pp. 223–227.
F. Maupain, "International Labour Organization Recommendations and Similar Instruments", in D. Shelton, ed., *Commitment and Compliance: The Role of Non-Binding Norms in the International Legal System*, Oxford, Oxford University Press, 2000, pp. 372–393.
ILO, *Demystifying the Core Conventions of the ILO through Social Dialogue: The Indonesian Experience*. Jakarta, ILO, 1999.
A. Trebilcock, "The ILO's Role in Supporting Asian Countries' Efforts to Respect Fundamental Principles and Rights at Work", paper presented to the International Industrial Relations Association, World Congress, Tokyo, 29 May–2 June 2000.
A. Trebilcock, "Trade, Labour Standards and Development: Challenges for Research from the Policy Consensus", paper presented to the Global Development Network, Bonn, December 1999.

Notes

1 The views expressed here are those of the author, not necessarily of the International Labour Office. The author gratefully acknowledges inputs from ILO colleagues John Ritchotte, who made the presentation to the Leuven group, and Patrick Carrière, who prepared a background paper for an earlier course.
2 ILO Declaration, para. 1(a). Note: the Declaration and related documents are available on the ILO website at http://mirror/public/eng/standards/decl/.

3   ILO Declaration, para. 1(b).
4   ILO Declaration, para. 2.
5   These are the Freedom of Association and Protection of the Right to Organize Convention, 1948 (No. 87), the Right to Organize and Collective Bargaining Convention, 1949 (No. 98), the Forced Labour Convention, 1930 (No. 29) and the Abolition of Forced Labour Convention, 1957 (No. 105), the Equal Remuneration Convention, 1951 (No. 100) and Discrimination (Employment and Occupation) Convention, 1958 (No. 111), and the Minimum Age Convention, 1973 (No. 138) and, since its unanimous adoption in 1999, the Worst Forms of Child Labour Convention, 1999 (No. 182), which will enter into force on 19 November 2000.
6   ILO Declaration, para. 3.
7   Ibid.
8   ILO Declaration, para. 5.
9   H. Kellerson, "The ILO Declaration of 1998 on Fundamental Principles and Rights: A Challenge for the Future", *International Labour Review*, 1998, Vol. 137, No. 2, pp. 223–227.
10 Memorandum of the United Nations Office of Legal Affairs, E/CN.4/L.610 (1962), 2 Apr. 1962.
11 The full text of the Follow-up appears as an Annex to the Declaration, and pursuant to paragraph 4 of that instrument, is an integral part of the Declaration.
12 ILO Constitution, Art. 19(5)(e), which provides for reporting on the position of a country's law and practice, showing the extent to which effect has been given given or is proposed to be given, to non-ratified Convnetions and stating the difficulties which prevent or delay ratification.
13 Until early 2001, countries not having any of the following Conventions are required to provide annual reports under the Declaration: Nos. 29, 87, 98, 100, 105, 111 and 138. Beginning in early 2001, annual reporting will extend to countries not having ratified the Worst Forms of Child Labour Convention, 1999 (No. 182), which is to enter into force on 19 November 2000 and is considered a fundamental Convention along with the seven others.
14 ILO Declaration, Annex, Para. II.A.1. The annual reports cover all four categories of principles and rights, but for each country only the ones relating to Conventions they have not ratified.
15 ILO Declaration, Annex, Para. II.B.1.
16 ibid., Para. II.B.3.
17 ibid., Para. III.A.1.
18 ILO, *Your Voice at Work*, Report of the Director-General, International Labour Conference, 88th Session, Report I(B), 2000. The debate appears in International Labour Conference, 88th Session, *Provisional Record* No. 11 (7 June 2000), and on the ILO website.
19 This report bears the number GB.279/TC/1, and will be available under the Conferences and Meetings icon of the general ILO website.
20 ILO Declaration, Annex, para. I. 2.
21 ILO, *Review of Annual Reports under the Follow-up to the ILO Declaration on Fundamental Principles and Rights at Work*, Part I, Introduction by the ILO Declaration Expert-Advisers to the Compilation of Annual Reports, GB.277/3/1, Mar. 2000, p. 1.
22 ILO, *ILO "core" Conventions ratifications surge past 1000 mark"*, Press Release, 22 September 2000 (http://mirror/public/english/bureau/inf/pr/2000/36.htm).
23 These points are explored more fully in A. Trebilcock, "The ILO's Role in Supporting Asian Countries' Efforts to Respect Fundamental Principles and Rights at Work", paper presented to the International Industrial Relations Association, World Congress, Tokyo, 29 May–2 June 2000.
24 This possibility is set out in ILO Declaration, Annex, para. IV.2.
25 Copenhagen Summit, Commitment 3(i), para. 54(b) of the Programme of Action.
26 ILO, "ILO "Core" Conventions Ratifications surge past 1000 Mark", Press Release, Sept. 2000.
27 OECD, *Trade, Employment and Labour Standards*, Paris 1996. An update is expected in 2000.
28 WTO, *Ministerial Declaration*, WT/MIN/(96)/DEC/W, para. 4,
29 International Labour Conference, 86th Session, 1998, *Provisional Record*, 1998, pp. 47–50.
30 F. Maupain, "International Labor Organization Recommendations and Similar Instruments", in

Anne Trebilcock

D. Shelton, *Commitment and Compliance: The Role of Non-Binding Norms in the International Legal System*, Oxford, Oxford University Press, 2000, p. 388.

31   ILO, *Decent Work*, International Labour Conference, 87th Session, Report I(a), 1999, p. 15.

32   *Your Voice at Work, supra*, pp. 23 and 46–47; ILO, *Demystifying the Core Conventions of the ILO through Social Dialogue: The Indonesian Experience*, 1999.

Janelle Diller

10. INTERNATIONAL LABOUR STANDARDS AND THE PRIVATE SECTOR

1. INTRODUCTION

Much attention is rightly given to the critical and central function of the ILO: standard setting and supervision of government obligations under Conventions and Recommendations. Like those instruments, the recent Declaration on Fundamental Principles and Rights at Work, adopted by the ILO in 1998, addresses the obligations of governments under the ILO Constitution and depends upon state reporting for its innovative follow up.

What is often set aside is the fact that the principles underlying those standards and the Declaration are actually implemented, and the benefits felt – or lack suffered – largely in private sector venues – in workplaces, families of workers, communities of operation. At primary level, the agents of change are individuals and groups of private actors – managers, employers and workers and their organisations, and community leaders, acting and interacting through social dialogue and other means of communication, organisation, and decision-making.

Traditionally, the supreme products of social dialogue are collective bargaining agreements. These bear unique and privileged status under many national legal systems, leading to supra-binding character and/or automatic or expedited enforceability where provided by law. Recently, products of such dialogue have been negotiated in transnational consultations and, in essence, represent agreements negotiated at international level between multinational enterprises (MNEs) and international trade secretariats or regional level employers' and workers' organisations. Unlike collective bargaining agreements concluded at national and local levels, these negotiated transnational agreements do not necessarily qualify for the privileged status given CBAs in many legal systems. Although the character and enforceability of these new agreements under national legal systems is a matter of continuing debate, surely they are enforceable under general contract law and procedures applicable in comparative jurisdiction. In certain countries they may be given added legal status, as reflected in the method of implementation of the 1997 agreement between the European Apparel

R. Blanpain and C. Engels (eds), The ILO and the Social Challenge of the 21st Century, 117–123.
© 2001 *Kluwer Law International. Printed in Great Britain.*

and Textile Organisation (EURATEX) and the European Trade Union Federation of Textiles, Clothing and Leather. Members composed of national level organisations have sought successfully in some cases to incorporate the agreement as a national level collective bargaining agreement, thus giving it equivalent legal status under national law to a collective agreement entered into between recognised trade unions and employers in the country.

Some codes of conduct and social labelling programs also represent results of dialogue between companies and workers, NGOs, consumers and shareholders. These typically convey public statements of commitments to certain social conduct made by corporate policy chiefs, undertaken on private voluntary initiative in context of corporate citizenship. What effect do such initiatives have in international and national law? At the least, they may be enforceable under commercial law principles, such as consumer claims of fraudulent misrepresentation of working conditions in their supply chains. Other private voluntary initiatives are program oriented; these include vocational training programs for workers, community health programs, and educational programs for former child workers.

These various initiatives result in part from a growing social awareness on the part of consumers and the press; enterprises may feel vulnerable to exposure of potentially abusive labour practices on the part of foreign business partners in commodity or service chains. They seek to establish social targets, or commitments to performance, across a production chain. Many of the targets commonly aim to reinforce or, in some cases, improve on existing legal requirements. Sometimes shareholders conduct initiatives seeking to institute codes of conduct in a particular enterprise, especially in the United States, Germany, Japan and other countries where laws and investment holdings permit.

2. POLICY FRAMEWORK

A review of the products generated by the private sector to publicly commit to methods of implementation of international labour standards raises several major questions from a policy point of view.

Question of Voluntariness
Private sector initiatives are considered to be voluntary in the sense that they are not directly required by law. Some enterprises and governments, particularly those in developing countries, contend that market pressure effectively renders such initiatives compulsory on terms and under processes which can be unfair. Developing countries may be implicated in private sector initiatives through contractual or corporate policy requirements imposed by multinational enterprises sourcing in the country. This argument should be considered in various aspects, including in the light of the content of the specific initiatives at issue and the method of corporate pressure used to obtain the "clean" conditions desired. To the extent the initiatives merely incorporate and go no further than the minimum threshold of internationally recognised core labour

standards, could this argument be justified? And what difference might it make were the MNE to seek a collaborative approach in its developing country linkages to build enterprise capacity in HRD and other management systems to meet the social specifications, rather than simply penalise by contract termination where specifications are not met? Related to this challenge to voluntariness are issues involving the transparency and participatory character of these initiatives, both in the development and implementation of the initiatives.

Question of Accountability
From a public policy perspective, self-regulation of the type reflected in codes and labels offers certain advantages. Some initiatives can promote corporate behaviour within the spirit of the law and thus complement public regulatory efforts, especially where public will or capacity is lacking. Some initiatives move beyond compliance requirements to serve as catalysts to advance law or policy beyond current thresholds that shape commercial behaviour. Yet risks and challenges are inherent arising from the private character and development of these initiatives outside traditional regulatory frameworks operating in ways that involve accountability to the public interest. Do the initiatives really result in achieving social justice and social and economic development through enjoyment of fundamental labour rights, better terms and conditions of work, and fuller employment? In sum, do they complement or compete with the aims and means of international labour standards and other international human rights law standards? And to whom are the actors accountable, if anyone? Are those most affected – workers and communities of operation – in a position to monitor, report and influence the effect of the initiatives?

3. RELATIONSHIP TO INTERNATIONAL LABOUR STANDARDS

The interaction between international labour standards, and derivatively the International Labour Organisation, and voluntary private initiatives was the subject of a Governing Body review and discussion in 1998 and 1999 based on a study of some 200 codes of conduct and a dozen operative social labelling programs.[1] The study analysed the content of the codes and labels addressing labour practices and in particular the core Declaration categories plus health and safety and wage levels. It also looked at the processes, principles and potential effects of such systems on the implementation and development of international labour standards.

Overall, the study concluded that the operation of private sector initiatives can complement, conflict, supplement or catalyse situations in which enforcement or progress is lacking. Specifically as to content, the initiatives born of purely private sector dynamics tended to be arbitrarily developed, based on the particular interests of those involved in the development. A high degree of selectivity of issues was involved: 75% of the codes reviewed covered health and safety; 66% discrimination, 40% child labour, 25% forced labour, and 15% freedom of association. The sources

119

or points of reference for definitions of the targets (e.g., "child labour", "discrimination") varied considerably. Most were based on self-definitions, some on national law, a few on industry practice, and only 1/3 even mentioned international standards. None mentioned the ILO Tripartite Declaration on Multinational Enterprises and Social Policy, a set of guidelines developed in 1977 that guides MNEs, workers, employers and governments around the world in maximising the benefits of multinational operations while minimising their adverse effects.

The study further found that, as to implementation, many systems with codes or labels lacked sufficient human resources, adequate worker participation, and support and assistance to developing country enterprises facing retailers' demands. Systems for assessing a company's performance were either through self-policing (with obvious disadvantages for credibility but based on need for confidentiality) and third party reporting (with problems of cost, access, especially in developing countries. No standardised methods for assessing performance have emerged in the market to date, although attempts have been made by private sector entities with diverse results. In contrast to financial auditing, social auditing has no generally accepted benchmarks for audit checklists or methodologies on how to review the books, talk with the workers.

4. NEW DIRECTIONS

From the study discussed in Part III and discussion within the ILO's executive policy organ, the Governing Body, came new questions and directions for ILO and the international system generally. Three of them are discussed below: (1) How can coherence be achieved in the content of these initiatives to permit complementarity and avoid conflict with public international standards, in particular international labour standards? In particular, could ILO standards serve as common benchmarks for conduct of private actors? (2) How can coherence be achieved in the implementation and assessment of these initiative? Social auditing is an unchartered profession; how can the impact both in the workplace, in communities, be accurately assessed, reported and compared across sectors and countries? (3) What role could the ILO usefully play on these issues?

4.1. Coherence in Content of Initiatives

This boils down to a concern for the coordination of public and private action, and specifically the role that international human rights law and international labour standards play. This is not a question of *Drittwirkung*, the legal proposition of direct regulation of private action at the international level (leaving aside the liability of private actors under international law for certain types of conduct proscribed as international crimes). Rather, the challenge is more reflective of the target posed by the UN Secretary General in 1999 in the UN Global Compact (copy in your readings), in calling global business actors to the international values reflected in the

Universal Declaration of Human Rights, the Declaration of Fundamental Principles and Rights at Work, and certain environmental standards. The ILO is a part of this Compact, as a core agency (along with UN Environmental Programme and the UN Office of the High Commissioner for Human Rights). As such, it is committed to assisting the growing group of multinationals which have publicly stated a resolve to promote these standards in their operations with suppliers and other linkages across global chains.

Other frameworks might also be helpful in addressing the normative coherence question, especially the multilateral "code" approach. In this area, two such codes predominate: the ILO Tripartite Declaration of Principles on Multinational Enterprises and Social Policy (MNE Declaration) and the OECD Guidelines on Multinational Enterprises.

4.1.1. MNE Declaration

At the multilateral level, the ILO's MNE Declaration uniquely addresses the universal commitments of four entities: MNEs, workers organisations, employers organisations, and governments. It has two main aims: to encourage the positive contribution which MNEs can make to economic and social progress, and to minimise and resolve the difficulties to which the very nature of their operations can give rise. The Declaration explicitly addresses human rights commitments by providing that all four parties should respect the Universal Declaration of Human Rights and the two international Covenants (International Covenant on Economic, Social and Cultural Rights and International Covenant on Civil and Political Rights). The range of topics addressed in the Declaration includes employment promotion and security, equality of opportunity and treatment, occupational health and safety, freedom of association and collective bargaining, and wages, benefits and conditions of work. The ILO Conventions and Recommendations which address the commitments of States on all these issues are annexed as relevant points of reference to the Declaration itself.

The effects of the application of the Tripartite Declaration are the subject of periodic surveys. These surveys examine both negative and positive effects of MNE activities based on information received from governments, workers, and employers. A Seventh Survey is in process, the results of which will be presented at the ILO's Governing Body meeting in March 2001. This seventh survey has enjoyed a greater response rate than any previous survey; replies from governments and social partners in 100 countries have been received. This Survey also covers special focuses, including linkages between MNEs and national enterprises, and the impact of MNE activities on lower income groups and developing areas and on the enjoyment of workers' rights in export processing and free trade zones. It is hoped that recommendations for action will take into account the leverage and resource-rich energy of voluntary private initiatives in ensuring the goals of the Tripartite Declaration are met in specific country and sectoral situations.

4.1.2. OECD Guidelines

The OECD's revised Guidelines on Multinational Enterprises have blazed a new path in incorporating much of the four core categories recognised in the ILO's 1998 Declaration on Fundamental Principles and Rights at Work into the non-binding commitments recommended by OECD Governments to their multinational enterprise operations around the world. The National Contact Points which are to be invigorated in overseeing the implementation of the Guidelines may provide new arenas for resolving disputes over social effects of the operation of multinationals of OECD home origin.

4.2. Coherence in Implementation of the Initiatives

This is largely an empirical question. The ILO is currently conducting research on how companies root codes in enterprise cultures, how they transfer expertise, and in particularly how they go about measuring and assessing the effects and values of those social policies.

4.3. Role of the ILO

To address the role of the ILO, a constitutional context-setting is helpful to understanding how social dialogue, private actors play a role in the ILO. In fact, ILO's experience is based on an 80-year history of social dialogue which is the heart of our identity as a tripartite organisation composed of governments, and representatives of national workers and employers organisations. The ILO operates in equal partnership between governments and the private sector "social partners" in drafting and adopting international standards, and in supervising and providing assistance to governments and other actors involved in implementing those standards. Although the Conventions and Recommendations bind only States members, they concern action to be taken by employers and workers. They are developed in a participatory and transparent system of rules and processes.

Based on this backdrop, and in keeping with the concern of the ILO to ensure that voluntary private initiatives complement international labour standards and principles, ILO has embarked on a multi-faceted programme of work in this area, including developing information and training resources and conducting projects in cooperation with industry. Its work in the UN Global Compact is part of this agenda.

4.3.1. Information Resources

As part of implementing its constitutional mandate to disseminate information, the International Labour Office is developing an electronic information clearing house on voluntary private initiatives as a service to business, labour, governments, and others concerned. This information bank of corporate codes, policies and practice guidelines will help provide an issues-based framework for socially responsible investment. In addition, ILO's website already features a page on "Business and Decent

Work",[2] which provides for synchronised links to search, by country and other fields, various knowledge bases of the ILO. These knowledge bases are highly relevant to socially responsible investor and enterprise conduct; topics include national labour laws, supervisory reviews and comments, surveys and interpretations of the ILO's MNE Declaration, and other guiding reference points, such as codes on health and safety, and training materials relevant to management systems.

4.3.2. Training Resources and Field Projects

Drawing on resources above, ILO is developing conventional and virtual training modules for use by business, labour, governments and others concerned that will encourage capacity and competence, at enterprise and sectoral level, to promote international labour principles through the use of voluntary private initiatives. ILO field projects bring together workers, employers, international investors and local business and community leaders to build capacity at enterprise and sectoral level to address challenges of socially responsible investment in the workplace and community. These have been pioneered in the child labour area, and are underway in projects implicating the other principles of the Declaration on Fundamental Principles and Rights at Work.

5. CONCLUSIONS

Much of the way ahead lies in uncharted territory. Some of that course lies through what has traditionally been considered corporate law areas; other aspects deal with public policy matters and still others implicate the relationship between private conduct and action based on publicly chartered mandates. It will be an exciting journey.

NOTES

1　The comprehensive study is found at ILO Doc. GB.273/WP/SDL/1 (1998).
2　See <http://www.ilo.org/public/english/comp/business/>.

123

David Kucera

11. DECENT WORK AND RIGHTS OF WORK: NEW MEASURES OF FREEDOM AND COLLECTIVE BARGAINING[1]

1. INTRODUCTION

In most general terms, the International Institute for Labour Studies' Decent Work research programme addresses the relationships among the ILO's four Decent Work strategic objectives: fundamental principles and rights at work; social protection; social dialogue; and employment and income opportunities. Within the ILO and elsewhere, there has long existed a range of competing hypotheses regarding the possible trade-offs and complementarities among these objectives. The Institute's research aims to more clearly understand the empirical and causal relationships among these objectives and the ways in which levels of development and country-specific institutions affect these relationships. The ultimate goal is to identify viable policies that could guide national and international strategies aimed at attaining Decent Work. For while Decent Work is clearly a desired end, identifying complementarities among the four strategic objectives suggests that Decent Work might also serve as a means to its own end, in a virtuous circle dynamic.

The first phase of this project looks at the relationship between fundamental rights at work and employment and income opportunities at the country level, beginning with the direction of causality running from the former to the latter. More specifically, measures of fundamental rights at work – freedom of association and collective bargaining, child labour, discrimination in employment, and forced labour – are being developed for use as explanatory variables in country-level econometric models of employment and income opportunities.[2] These initial directions of causality explored are illustrated by the bold arrows in Figure 1.

The hypotheses regarding the causal relationship from fundamental rights at work to employment and income opportunities have been surveyed elsewhere and are not discussed in any detail in this paper (e.g. Rodrik 1996). But the basic hypothesis is that greater rights at work might lead to higher labour costs per worker hour, whether through higher wages or higher non-wage labour costs. This might lead then to higher

R. Blanpain and C. Engels (eds), The ILO and the Social Challenge of the 21st Century, 125–135.
© 2001 *Kluwer Law International. Printed in Great Britain.*

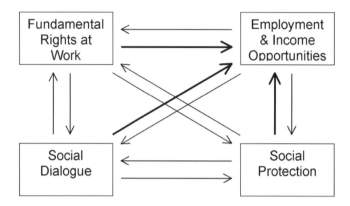

Figure 1. Causal relations among the four strategic objectives

labour costs per unit of output, depending on the effects of greater rights at work on labour productivity. These hypothesised causal connections vary for different rights at work, as different rights represent phenomena of fundamentally different natures. These differences will be explored in considerable detail in a forthcoming literature survey, but the general hypothesis noted here provides a rough and ready starting point. As for the effects of changes in unit labour costs on changes in other aspects of employment and income opportunities, this depends on a range of mediating factors, such as price elasticities of demand for goods as well as micro-cost factors and macro-demand factors that might pull in opposite directions. These and other issues, theoretical and empirical, will also be explored in the survey paper.

A key bottleneck in this research is the lack of quality measures of fundamental rights at work. As the World Bank Development Research Group puts it, "Available measures of labor standards are questionable indicators of actual worker rights and could be improved" (Martin and Maskus 1999). Similar views have been put forth by Richard Freeman (1996) and the OECD (1996). First on the Institute's task list then is the development of improved measures of rights at work.

This paper presents the Institute's work to date on its measure of freedom of association and collective bargaining. The Institute's measure is presented in the context of generally desirable properties of "subjective" statistical indicators and of a comparison with an important previously-developed measure of freedom of association/collective bargaining constructed by the OECD (1996). The paper is structured as follows. First, the paper defines four desirable properties of "subjective" statistical indicators. The paper then describes the OECD's and Institute's measures, looking at the definition used in construction, information sources used, and methods of construction. The two indicators are then evaluated according to four desirable properties of "subjective" statistical indicators. The paper concludes with suggestions for further work. It is argued that there is value in having multiple approaches of measuring of freedom of association/collective bargaining, as well as of other fundamental rights at work. For different approaches have their own strengths and weaknesses, and the relationship between rights at work and other desired outcomes could be more definitively understood through the use of multiple measures.

2. Desirable Properties of "Subjective" Statistical Indicators

"Subjective" statistical indicators are those constructed from assigning numerical values to qualitative information, usually text. More commonly used are "objective" indicators based on pre-existing numerical data (Bollen and Paxton 2000). Regarding freedom of association/collective bargaining, objective indicators could include unionisation and collective bargaining coverage rates. It is worth noting that the subjective versus objective distinction has a technical meaning in this context and does not accord strictly with the more general definition of subjective and objective. For so-called objective indicators, such as price indices and estimates of capital stock, typically involve varying degrees of subjective judgement in their construction. And so-called subjective indicators also vary in the degree of subjective judgment used to construct them.

Four important properties of subjective indicators are *accuracy, reproducibility, transparency* (closely related to reproducibility), *sufficient grades of variation*, and *accuracy*. These are briefly defined as follows.

Reproducibility: Will different evaluators be able to consistently reproduce each other's results?

Transparency: How systematic and obvious is the rating method? How well can a score be traced back to individual sources of information?

Sufficient grades of variation: Is the indicator sufficiently finely graded to capture important dimensions of variation in the concept it aims to measure?

Accuracy: How well does the indicator measure the phenomena it aims to measure?

There are several potential sources of inaccuracy, each leading to systematic (as opposed to random) measurement error. Among these are whether the definition used to construct the indicator is conceptually consistent with what one aims to measure; whether there is a bias in the sources of information used to construct the indicator; and whether the evaluators constructing the indicator are biased, consistently pre-judging certain groups of countries (Bollen and Paxton 2000).

Regarding the use of measures of rights at work, the Institute's basic strategy is twofold: to rely on both subjective and objective indicators whenever appropriate and possible; and to build on the related conditions of reproducibility and transparency. Regarding the latter, the Institute's approach differs from that of the OECD's, for which ratings rely on the more impressionistic judgement of a panel of experts. The rationale for the Institute's emphasis on reproducibility and transparency is the same as for empirical work and experimental design in general, that different researchers should be able to reconstruct other researchers' results. More than that, satisfying the

David Kucera

conditions of reproducibility and transparency lessens an important source of systematic measurement error – the bias of evaluators. In an important recent study, Bollen and Paxton provide strong evidence that evaluator bias is a significant source of systematic measurement error for a number of subjective indicators of liberal democracy (2000). That is, evaluators are biased by what Bollen and Paxton call "situational closeness", the extent to which a country is more or less like their own. Satisfying the conditions of transparency and reproducibility, then, can also be a means of improving accuracy.

3. The OECD's Indicator of Freedom of Association/Collective Bargaining

In constructing its indicator of freedom of association/collective bargaining, the OECD bases its definition on ILO Conventions 87 (Freedom of Association and Protection of the Right to Organise, of 1948) and 98 (Right to Organise and Collective Bargaining, of 1949). The OECD uses three main information sources: the International Confederation of Free Trade Unions (ICFTU) *Annual Survey of Violations of Trade Union Rights*; the U.S. State Department's *Country Reports on Human Rights Practices*; and the ILO's *ILOLEX*, an electronic database of relevant ILO documents. Compared with the other fundamental rights at work, the sources of textual information for freedom of association/collective bargaining are relatively rich. The ICFTU and U.S. State Department reports are particularly well suited for the creation of subjective indicators, as they are structured as annual country reports and are available for a wide range of countries.

In terms of definitions and especially information sources, the OECD's and Institute's indicators are similar. As such, the measures do not differ in terms of these two key sources of systematic measurement error noted above. Where the OECD and Institute indicators differ considerably is in methods of construction. The OECD's method involves creating a table with up to a paragraph of text for each of three categories: restrictions on the right to establish free unions; restrictions on the right to strike; and protection of union members and collective bargaining rights. Based on these three tables, a panel of evaluators gives each country an overall score (not a score for each of the three categories) of 1, 2, 3 or 4, with 1 indicating strongest rights and 4 indicating weakest rights. Regarding the classification of countries as well as the criteria used for classification, the OECD writes:

> Based on the above information [qualitative descriptions in the three tables], it is now possible to arrange countries in different groups, based on [OECD] Secretariat judgement concerning the extent to which they comply with freedom of association. In group 1, comprising all OECD countries (except Mexico and Turkey), as well as the Bahamas, Barbados, Israel, Malta, and Surinam, freedom of association is by and large guaranteed in law and practice. At the other

128

extreme are group 4 countries, where freedom of association is practically non-existent (China, Egypt, Indonesia, Iran, Kuwait, Syria and Tanzania). In countries of group 2 (Argentina, Brazil, Chile, Ecuador, Ethiopia, Fiji, Hong Kong, India, Jamaica, Mexico, Niger, Papua New Guinea, Peru, South Africa, Venezuela and Zambia) some restrictions exist, but it is possible to establish independent workers' organisations and union confederations. In the remaining group of countries (group 3), restrictions on freedom of association are significant: the existence of stringent registration requirements, political interference or acts of anti-union discrimination make it very difficult to form independent workers' organisations or union confederations (OECD 1996: 43).

Using these methods, the OECD constructed its freedom of association/collective bargaining indicator for a total of seventy-five countries, based on information for the early to mid-1990s. The descriptive tables used to construct the indicators were recently updated by the OECD, based on information for the middle to late 1990s (2000).

4. The Institute's Indicator of Freedom of Association/Collective Bargaining

The Institute's indicator of freedom of association/collective bargaining uses the same three main information sources as the OECD indicator. The definition used is also similar to that of the OECD and is based on ILO Conventions 87 and 98 and related ILO jurisprudence. In addition, the Institute's definition is based on the range of *de facto* and *de jure* problems described in the information sources. In this sense, the Institute's definition unfolded from an interaction between *a priori* considerations based on ILO documents as well as considerations of problems of a more everyday nature.

The OECD's and Institute's measures differ most in the method of construction. The Institute's measure is based on thirty-seven evaluation criteria, which provide a detailed working definition of freedom of association/collective bargaining. That is, while the OECD's and Institute's definitions of freedom of association/collective bargaining are similar in broad conceptual terms, the Institute's definition is considerably more explicit. This spelling out of the definition, component by component, informs the Institute's method of construction.

The Institute's method of construction consists of the following steps. First, the information sources are examined country-by-country for a given period. Problems found regarding the thirty-seven evaluation criteria are then coded with letters "a", "b", or "c", indicating the information source. Next a dummy variable is constructed for each country in which an observation of a problem in any of the three information sources and is given a value of 1 and no observations in any of the three sources is given a value of 0, for each of the evaluation criteria. Each of the evaluation criteria is assigned a weight of 1, 1.25, 1.5, 1.75 or 2, with higher weights indicating more severe

129

problems. The indicator will also be constructed without any weights and then econometric models tested with both weighted and un-weighted indicators to assess the extent to which the weighting scheme affects regression results. Dummy variables for each country are then multiplied by the weights, with this product summed across the evaluation criteria to yield, for each country, a non-normalised score. Lower scores are taken to indicate greater rights of freedom of association/collective bargaining and higher scores the opposite.

There are, no doubt, elements of subjectivity (in the conventional sense) in determining the thirty-seven evaluation criteria and in assigning weights, but these judgements are all made explicit. One advantage of the Institute's approach is that different researchers could use different subsets of the thirty-seven evaluation criteria as well as their own weighting schemes, depending on their own judgements and research and policy concerns. One could also use endogenous weighting methods to derive freedom of association/collective bargaining indicators from its thirty-seven individual components, such as principle components analysis. In more general terms, the aim of the project is not to construct the definitive measure of freedom of association/collective bargaining. Rather, the strategy is to evaluate the extent to which different measures constructed from different methods affect the understanding of the relationships between rights at work and other desired outcomes.

The Institute's method is illustrated in Table 1 for sample country X in the mid-1990s (based on problems occurring in the five-year period from 1993 and 1997). Column 1 shows the thirty-seven evaluation criteria grouped by six categories: freedom of association/collective bargaining-related civil liberties; right to establish and join union and worker organisations; other union activities; right to collectively bargain; right to strike; and export processing zones. It should be emphasised that the descriptions of the thirty-seven evaluation criteria listed in column are simply labels, not definitions. Each of the evaluation criteria is described in considerable detail in a set of definitions and decision rules, indicating relevant ILO Convention articles and jurisprudence passages; how to classify the diverse range of problems noted in the information sources; and how the various evaluation criteria relate to each other (in terms of mutual exclusivity, whether a single problem implies more than one evaluation criteria, and so on). The aim is to have a sufficiently detailed set of definitions and decision rules that different evaluators would attain the same (or at least very similar) results. That is, the aim is reproducibility.

Column 2 shows the coding of problems according to the information source and column 3 the dummy variables derived from column 2. Within column 3, a look at the two shaded rows indicates a value in the dummy variable of 1 for both rows, even though problems were found in all three information sources for the upper row and only one source for the lower row. The rationale for treating both rows the same (rather than giving more weight to the upper) is that the different sources are often describing the same problem in a country. Indeed, the State Dept. reports are based in part on the ICFTU reports and information from the ILO, and the ICFTU reports are in turn based in part on information from the ILO.

Weights are shown in column 4 as unknowns, since the weighting scheme will be finalised based on additional consultation with ILO colleagues. Column 5 shows the product of the dummy and the weights, the sum of which yields the non-normalised score for a given country. The unweighted score is simply the sum of column 3. Endogenous weighting methods can be constructed using in the information in both columns 3 and 5.

At present, the indicators are being constructed for roughly 175 countries for the mid-1990s for use in cross-sectional models. Panel data models enable the analysis of change over time, including change solely within countries over time (in fixed effects models). Using countries as observations, panel data models are commonly constructed using five-year intervals, such as for years 1990, 1995, and so on; or using five-year averages, such as for years 1988 to 1992, 1993 to 1997, and so on. The textual information sources are of considerably lower quality prior to the mid-1990s, complicating the construction of the freedom of association/collective bargaining measure for earlier years. It is planned, though, that the measure will be updated along with the information sources used in their construction, enabling the study of change from the mid-1990s onward.

5. Comparing Desirable Properties

How do the OECD's and Institute's measures rate in terms of the four desirable properties noted above?

Reproducibility. The OECD's indicator seems less readily reproducible than the Institute's indicator. One can test for reproducibility, of course, and the Institute will conduct such tests in the course of its research programme.

Transparency. Since the Institute's indicator is more explicit about the determinants of the scoring process, it would seem to rank higher than the OECD's indicator in terms of transparency. The Institute's measure also enables one to trace back a score to its individual components and individual sources of information. In this sense, the Institute's measure is more contestable, more readily subject to review.

Sufficient grades of variation. As it is based on thirty-seven evaluation criteria, the Institute's measure has a fairly wide range of variability compared with the OECD's four-category classification. The OECD measure gives all OECD countries aside from Mexico and Turkey the same high score of 1, but rights of freedom of association and collective bargaining appear to vary considerably among these countries. It is reasonable to question whether these variations in freedom of association/collective bargaining could contribute to differences in wages and labour costs and through these other aspects of employment and income opportunities. In this sense, the OECD's measure does not seem sufficiently finely graded to capture important dimensions of the underlying concept it aims to measure.

Accuracy. As the OECD and Institute use similar definitions and information sources, they rate the same in terms of these sources of systematic measurement error. It could be that the information sources used are biased. For instance, it could be that

131

David Kucera

Table 1: Institute's Measure of Freedom of Association/Collective Bargaining, Country X in mid-1990s

[1] 37 Evaluation Criteria	[2] Sources	[3] Dummy (0=no evidence, 1=evidence)	[4] Weights (1, 1.25, 1.5, 1.75 or 2)	[5] Dummy*Weights
A. Freedom of association/collective bargaining-related civil liberties				
Murder or disappearance of union members or organizers		0	$w1$	0
Other violence against union members or organizers	ab	1	$w2$	$w2$
Arrest, detention, imprisonment, or forced exile for union membership or activities	a	1	$w3$	$w3$
Interference with union rights of assembly, demonstration, free opinion, free expression	ab	1	$w4$	$w4$
Seizure or destruction of union premises or property		0	$w5$	0
B. Right to establish and join union and worker organizations				
General prohibitions		0	$w6$	0
General absence resulting from socio-economic breakdown		0	$w7$	0
Previous authorization requirements		0	$w8$	0
Employment conditional on non-membership in union		0	$w9$	0
Dismissal or suspension for union membership or activities	abc	1	$w10$	$w10$
Interference of employers (attempts to dominate unions)	a	1	$w11$	$w11$
Dissolution or suspension of union by administrative authority		0	$w12$	0
Only workers' committees & labour councils permitted		0	$w13$	0
Only state-sponsored or other single unions permitted		0	$w14$	0
Exclusion of tradeable/industrial sectors from union membership		0	$w15$	0
Exclusion of other sectors or workers from union membership	ab	1	$w16$	$w16$
Other specific de facto problems or acts of prohibition	a	1	$w17$	$w17$
Right to establish and join federations or confederations of unions		0	$w18$	0
Previous authorization requirements regarding above row		0	$w19$	0
C. Other union activities				
Right to elect representatives in full freedom	ab	1	$w20$	$w20$
Right to establish constitutions and rules		0	$w21$	0
General prohibition of union/federation participation in political activities	b	1	$w22$	$w22$
Union control of finances	c	1	$w23$	$w23$

D. Right to collectively bargain

General prohibitions		0	w24	0
Prior approval by authorities of collective agreements		0	w25	0
Compulsory binding arbitration		0	w26	0
Intervention of authorities		0	w27	0
Scope of collective bargaining restricted by non-state employers		0	w28	0
Exclusion of tradeable/industrial sectors from right to collectively bargain		0	w29	0
Exclusion of other sectors or workers from right to collectively bargain	ab	1	w30	w30
Other specific de facto problems or acts of prohibition	ab	1	w31	w31

E. Right to strike

General prohibitions		0	w32	0
Previous authorization required by authorities		0	w33	0
Exclusion of tradeable/industrial sectors from right to strike		0	w34	0
Exclusion of other sectors or workers from right to strike	ab	1	w35	w35
Other specific de facto problems or acts of prohibition	ac	1	w36	w36

F. Export Processing Zones

Restricted rights in EPZ'S	a	1	w37	w37

Non-normalized score: *sum of above*

Sources

a: International Confederation of Free Trade Unions (ICFTU), *Annual Survey of Violations of Trade Union Rights* .
b: U.S. State Department, *Country Reports on Human Rights Practices.*
c: ILO, *ILOLEX* .

133

there is simply more information available for larger, English-speaking countries, and that this would translate into systematic measurement error. This potential problem is worth exploring, and Bollen and Paxton have developed a test for such bias as well as suggestions for correction (Bollen and Paxton 2000). It is worth noting though that bias in information sources was not found to be an important source of systematic measurement error for the several subjective indicators of liberal democracy evaluated by Bollen and Paxton.

Regarding the bias of evaluators, it was noted above that the Institute's indicator seems less vulnerable to such problems, for the measure better satisfies the conditions of reproducibility and transparency. If the above were all that mattered, the preferability of the Institute's measure would be clearcut. But other factors come are also important. For while the OECD's approach appears less readily reproducible and less transparent, it allows room for more nuanced judgements than the Institute's approach. Consider the problem of dismissal for union activities. The Institute's measure treats one dismissal the same as a thousand dismissals. The OECD approach need not. Put in more general terms, there appears to be a trade-off between satisfying the conditions of reproducibility and transparency and the amount of room for nuanced judgements. Because it leaves more room for nuanced judgements, the OECD approach might also enable one to more accurately measure latent rights of freedom of association/collective bargaining, in contrast with the Institute's approach in which rights are measured by their manifest absence. More generally, different approaches have different strengths and weaknesses, and the study of relationships between rights at work and other desired outcomes would be deepened through the use of multiple approaches and measures.

6. CONCLUSION: SUGGESTIONS FOR FURTHER WORK

The basic approach taken by the OECD could be improved on the use of a greater number of evaluation criteria. Useful models in this regard are the Freedom House indicators of civil liberties and political rights. These measures are constructed by a panel of evaluators giving a score of 0, 1, 2, 3, or 4 for each of seven categories, with the total scores derived by summing across the seven categories (Freedom House 1999). Modifying the OECD approach in this manner would certainly create more grades of variation and would also likely improve transparency and reproducibility.

Regarding the Institute's approach, it seems likely that the trade-off between reproducibility and transparency on the one hand and nuanced judgements on the other could be lessened through improved information sources. In particular, it would be useful if the process of constructing indicators were better integrated with the collection of information. Such integration seems a promising strategy for improving the accuracy of subjective indicators of rights at work, for it would enable a more exact match between the definitions used to construct indicators and to collect information.

Bibliography

Bollen, Kenneth and Pamela Paxton. 2000. "Subjective Measures of Liberal Democracy". *Comparative Political Studies* 33(1): 58–86.

Freedom House. 1999. *Freedom in the World: The Annual Survey of Political Rights and Civil Liberties, 1998–1999*. New York: Freedom House.

Freeman, Richard. 1996. "International Labor Standards and World Trade: Friends or Foes?" in Jeffrey Schott (ed.) *The World Trading System: Challenges Ahead*. Washington, D.C.: Institute for International Economics.

Martin, Will and Keith Maskus. 1999. "Core Labor Standards and Competitiveness: Implications for Global Trade Policy". World Bank Development Research Group Report (Draft, October 4).

OECD. 1996. *Trade, Employment and Labour Standards: A Study of Core Workers' Rights and International Trade*. Paris: Organisation for Economic Cooperation and Development.

OECD. 2000. *An Update of the 1996 Study "Trade, Employment and Labour Standards: A Study of Core Workers' Rights and International Trade"*. Paris: Organisation for Economic Cooperation and Development.

Rodrik, Dani. 1996. "Labor Standards in International Trade: Do They Matter and What Do We Do About Them?" in Robert Lawrence, Dani Rodrik, and John Whalley (eds.) *Emerging Agenda for Global Trade: High Stakes for Developing Countries*. Washington, D.C.: Overseas Development Council.

Notes

1   This paper is based on a presentation given by the author at the International Conference on Statistics, Development and Human Rights sponsored by the International Association for Official Statistics (IAOS) (Montreux, September 2000). The paper benefited from comments by participants at the IAOS conference, by Ludovic Lebart, and by a number of ILO colleagues, especially Richard Anker, Lucio Baccaro, Eivind Hoffmann, Farhad Mehran and Gerhard Reinecke.

2   For the time being, the variables providing a working definition of employment and income opportunities are wages and labour costs, foreign direct investment, comparative trade advantage, employment growth, and output growth, these being the dependent variables of the econometric models. Foreign direct investment and comparative trade advantage are considered not only because they can lead to, under the right conditions, employment and income opportunities; they are considered also because they represent key aspects of globalisation, an important subject of ILO policy concern.

Frank Hagemann

12. ACTION AGAINST CHILD LABOUR:
AN INTERNATIONAL PERSPECTIVE

Child labour challenges our sense of decency and humanity. It is a gruesome reality all over the world. No continent is free of it. We find in small villages and in big cities, in the lanes of destitute slums and on the brightly-lit boulevards of our capitals. The magnitude of the problem is indeed enormous. At least 250 million children have to go to work each day.[1] Half of them are working all day long, in many cases 12 to 15 hours a day. The problem is most acute in Asia, where most of the world's child labourers live, and Africa, where roughly 40 per cent of all children have to work. But it is also an important problem in Latin America. ILO numbers show that one out of six children is working on this continent. Moreover, child labour also still exists in industrialised countries[2] and has been reappearing in the transition economies of Eastern and Central Europe.

Yet statistics are abstract and tend to speak a cold language. There is pain behind these numbers. For the consequences of child labour are serious, sometimes even fatal. Most child workers miss childhood and grow up with no time for school or play. Millions of children risk their health and lives in hazardous occupations, in prostitution, or are exploited as virtual slaves.

The employment of very young children and of girls is a particularly alarming problem. The younger the children, the more vulnerable they are to hazards at the workplace and to economic exploitation. ILO survey results show that in some areas up to 20 per cent of child workers are under the age of ten. The situation of the girl child deserves particular attention. There are two reasons for concern. The first is the sheer number: ILO estimates suggest that there are at least 110 million girl child workers and this number does not even include those who work in their own parents' household. The second concern is the nature of work girls are involved in. Much of their work is hidden from public view. Many girls are found in some of the worst kinds and conditions of work such as commercial sexual exploitation. Child domestic service is another area of major concern. Girls working as child domestics are largely invisible workers, dispersed and mostly ignored. Isolated away from home and sometimes virtually enslaved, they are often exposed to violence and sexual abuse.

The picture is indeed sobering and one may be tempted to express pessimism in the

R. Blanpain and C. Engels (eds), The ILO and the Social Challenge of the 21st Century, 137–142.
© *2001 Kluwer Law International. Printed in Great Britain.*

137

face of such enormous child exploitation. However, we are happy to be able to contradict the pessimists among us. In spite of the huge extent of the problem and the depth of abuse there are grounds for being optimistic. Let me explain why.

One of the most striking developments over the last few years has been the remarkable change of attitudes and perceptions in regard to child labour. It has to be recalled that for a long time child labour had been tolerated and accepted as part of the natural order of things. Only a decade ago child labour was often condoned in silence. This is no longer the case. Within a relatively short time, child labour has advanced from being a side issue among global political, economic and social preoccupations to become a high priority on the agenda of the world community. Governments and civil society show a hitherto unknown determination to address the problem on all fronts.

This is reflected in the growing number of countries seeking assistance from the ILO's International Programme on the Elimination of Child Labour (IPEC), a programme which helps countries develop and undertake practical action against child labour and to which I shall revert below.

It is reflected in the determination of governments from all over the world who adopted unanimously, in June 1999 in Geneva, a new international human rights instrument on child labour, the ILO's *Worst Forms of Child Labour Convention (No. 182)*. Only sixteen months later, this Convention had already been ratified by 43 countries (October 2000). Convention 182 has the fastest ratification pace in the ILO's 81-year history and there is expectation that it will soon be universally ratified.

It is also reflected in the commitment of thousands of individuals, groups and non-governmental organisations who have carried the torch and transformed what was at best a fledging local concern into a formidable worldwide movement. The best and most inspiring example of this was the Global March Against Child Labour,[3] which culminated with the extraordinary entrance of child workers from all over the world at the ILO's International Labour Conference in Geneva in 1998, appealing for the adoption of a new Convention that would prohibit and put an end to the worst forms of child labour.

And it is reflected in the fact that child labour is becoming a consumer concern in both developing and industrialised countries. Corporations are reacting to campaigns by human rights and consumer groups demanding corporate responsibility from manufacturers to respect human rights, including the ILO's Conventions on workers' rights and child labour. World-renowned manufacturers are now looking into the conditions under which their products are being produced.

These are very significant and encouraging developments. But there is hardly any doubt that there is still a long way to go. Change will always only be gradual and the very recognition of this fact should guide action and approaches on child labour. Given this, what can and should be done to bring about the eventual elimination of child labour ? Three steps seem to be essential to me:

• to aim at the rapid and universal ratification and application of the new ILO Convention on the worst forms of child labour;

- to develop strong national policies and time-bound programmes of action on child labour, giving primacy to preventive measures including the provision of free, universal and compulsory education; and
- to strengthen political will and civil society's resolve to act against child labour.

I should point out that the three steps are not a sequence. Each one is important in its own right. All of them are a priority. I shall briefly explain them.

First, there is a need to achieve a quick and hopefully universal ratification of the Worst Forms of Child Labour Convention. Before coming to the details of this Convention, let me briefly give you the background. The ILO is a standard-setting organisation and since its foundation in 1919 it has adopted several international labour standards specifying the minimum age of entry to employment or work and defining the conditions under which children may be allowed to work. The most comprehensive ILO instrument on child labour is the Minimum Age Convention No. 138, adopted in 1973.[4] Its cornerstone is the requirement that ratifying States undertake to pursue a national policy designed to ensure the effective abolition of child labour. They also have to raise the minimum age for admission to employment or work to a level consistent with the fullest physical and mental development of young persons. The Convention establishes that the minimum age should not be less than the age of compulsory schooling and in no event less than 15 years of age. A number of exceptions are granted to developing countries. At the end of October 2000, 102 countries had ratified Convention No.138.

The number of ratifications has lately been sharply increasing. We expect it to rise further in the coming years. An important impetus had been given by the ILO's Declaration on Fundamental Principles and Rights at Work, adopted in 1998. The Declaration states that all Members have an obligation arising from the very fact of membership in the Organisation, to respect, promote and realise certain fundamental labour principles including the effective abolition of child labour.[5]

While Convention No.138 remains the fundamental international standard on child labour, there was growing international consensus that there are certain forms of child labour that cannot be tolerated under any circumstances, no matter how developed or poor a country is.

As a result, a new Convention and Recommendation (C.182 and R.190, respectively) were put forward by the ILO's 174 member States and adopted last year. The new Convention requires ratifying States to take immediate and effective measures to prohibit and eliminate the worst forms of child labour as a matter of urgency for all those under 18 years of age.[6]

The *"worst forms of child labour"* include:

(a) all forms of slavery or practices similar to slavery, such as the sale and trafficking of children, debt bondage and serfdom and forced or compulsory labour, including forced or compulsory recruitment of children for use in armed conflict;

(b)   the use, procurement or offering of a child for prostitution, production of pornography or pornographic performances; and for illicit activities, in particular
for the production and trafficking of drugs; and

(c)   work which, by its nature or the circumstances in which it is carried out, is likely
to harm the health, safety or morals of children.

The latter is commonly referred to as hazardous work. No detailed definition of
this is in the Convention but it is instead left to the ratifying States to determine what
constitutes hazardous work. States must formulate a detailed list of dangerous work
and the Recommendation accompanying Convention No. 182 provides further guidance for States on which types of work to consider. It suggests:

- work which exposes children to physical, psychological or sexual abuse;
- work underground, under water, at dangerous heights or in confined spaces;
- work with dangerous machinery, equipment and tools, or which involves the
manual handling or transport of heavy loads;
- work in an unhealthy environment which may, for example, expose children to
hazardous substances, agents or processes, or to temperatures, noise levels, or
vibrations damaging to their health; and
- work under particularly difficult conditions such as work for long hours or during
the night or work where the child is unreasonably confined to the premises of the
employer.

Effective enforcement and implementation of the Convention are important to
ensure that law is turned into practice. The Convention requires not only effective
enforcement measures, including penal sanctions, but also requires national monitoring mechanisms to be established. These mechanisms could, for example, be national
committees or advisory bodies on child labour. They could also be designed to
oversee a particular sector such as the informal sector, where many children often
work, but where institutions such as labour inspection cannot easily reach them.

An interesting aspect of the Convention and Recommendation is that they take a
very action oriented approach to child labour. It is clear that laws alone cannot
eradicate the worst forms of child labour. That is why the instruments promote
dynamic and comprehensive action calling for both effective measures to be taken
and programmes of action to be designed and implemented. Taking an action-ori-
ented approach to child labour requires the participation of a wide group of actors.
The instruments require consultation with employers' and workers' organisations,
but in addition to the ILO tripartite constituency, the instruments also call for
consideration to be given to the views of other concerned groups, including the views
of children directly affected by the worst forms of child labour and their families,
when designing and implementing programmes of action.

Finally, the Convention calls for member States to cooperate and assist each other
to effectively prohibit and eliminate the worst forms of child labour. Most of the

international cooperation on child labour is delivered through the before-mentioned ILO's International Programme on the Elimination of Child Labour, or IPEC in short. IPEC started in 1992 and it has over the years blossomed into one of the world's largest technical cooperation programmes, a 90-country global action alliance against child labour. This includes more than 60 countries on four continents where the ILO is carrying out cutting-edge field programmes and bringing together a broad alliance of interests, encompassing government, trade unions, employers groups, non-governmental organisations and many others. The programme is inspiring, guiding and supporting national initiatives against child labour in such important areas as policy-making, legislative reform, data collection, research and awareness-raising. From the outset, IPEC places emphasis on countries taking ownership of action against child labour in order to ensure long-term sustainability.[7]

This year, IPEC is embarking on what is perhaps its most ambitious venture to date. On a pilot basis, a number of countries on three continents will be assisted to implement large time-bound programmes against child labour. The goal is eradicate the worst forms of child labour within a clearly defined time-frame. Massive resources will be needed and are now forthcoming, both from within the countries and from a committed donor community.

Strong political will is essential to the success of these programmes, and indeed of any action against child labour. Governments ultimately have the prime responsibility in the fight against child labour. But civil society can act as an important watchdog, fighting against public apathy and fostering and sustaining the government's political will to take action against the scourge of child labour.

Workers and employers and their organisations have an important role to play in supporting these efforts.[8] Unions are the logical leaders for exposing and denouncing child labour abuses. They can become credible advocates for the rights of children to education while at the same time asserting the rights of adult workers to adequate remuneration, thereby reducing the dependency of poor families on child labour. The business community can also contribute to the fight against child labour and is increasingly doing so, realising that child labour can taint a corporate image and impede business success.

As shown above, work against child labour has made important progress over the last few years. Yet there is no time for complacency. On the contrary, efforts will have to intensified at all levels in order to achieve what the world's children are waiting for. While child labour is essentially a national problem which calls for national solutions, there is an important role for the international community and indeed international solidarity and cooperation. Without joint action and international cooperation it would be virtually impossible to stop the trafficking and economic exploitation of children in forced and hazardous work, in prostitution and in pornography.

Moreover, while poverty cannot be an excuse for inaction against the worst forms of child labour, it must nonetheless be addressed if we are to deal with the problem of child labour on a sustained basis. The problem is primarily a national responsibility, and national governments must design policies and programmes aimed at providing

141

productive employment attacking poverty. But it is also a world responsibility. Increased efforts will have to be made at the international level to see in what way the world community could be mobilised in a sustained attack on the main underlying causes of child labour, namely poverty and the causes of poverty such as unemployment, underemployment and social exclusion.

NOTES

1   For these and other child labour statistics, see Ashagrie, A., *Statistics on working children and hazardous child labour in brief*, International Labour Office, Geneva. First published 1997, revised April 1998. Results of the ILO's child labour surveys, including micro-data, are to be found on www.ilo.org/childlabour

2   See Dorman, P., *Child labour in developed economies*, ILO/IPEC working paper, Geneva (forthcoming)

3   For comprehensive information on the Global March and its activities, see www.globalmarch.org

4   For the full text of the Convention, see www.ilo.org/public/english/standards/ipec/publ/law/ilc/c1381973.

5   See www.ilo.org/public/english/standards/decl for the full text of and comprehensive information on the Declaration.

6   For the full text of the Convention, see www.ilo.org/public/english/standards/ipec/ratification/convention/text.htm

7   See www.ilo.org/public/english/standards/ipec for more information on IPEC's partners, activities and approaches.

8   For examples and guidance on action see, amongst others, Haspels, N., Jankanish, M., *Action against child labour*, ILO Geneva 2000

INDEX

147

Index

STUDIES IN EMPLOYMENT AND SOCIAL POLICY

1. W. Beck, L. van der Maesen and A. Walker (eds.): *The Social Quality of Europe*. 1997
    ISBN 90-411-0456-9

2. F. Pennings: *Introduction to European Social Security Law*. 2001
    ISBN 90-411-1628-1

3. R. Blanpain, M. Colucci, C. Engels, F. Hendrickx, L. Salas and J. Wouters:
    Institutional Changes and European Social Policies after the Treaty of Amsterdam. 1998
    ISBN 90-411-1018-6

4. Vai Io Lo: *Law and Industrial Relations: China and Japan after World War II*. 1998
    ISBN 90-411-1075-5

5. A. den Exter and H. Hermans (eds.): *The Right to Health Care in Several European
    Countries*. 1999   ISBN 90-411-1087-9

6. M. Biagi (ed.): *Job Creation and Labour Law: from protection towards pro-action*. 2000
    ISBN 90-411-1432-7

7. W. Beck, L.J.G. van der Maesen, F. Thomése and A. Walker (eds.): *Social Quality:
    A Vision for Europe*. 2000   ISBN 90-411-1523-4

8. J. Murray (ed.): *Transnational Labour Regulation: The ILO and EU Compared*. 2001
    ISBN 90-411-1583-8

9. R. Blanpain and C. Engels (eds.): *The ILO and the Social Challenges of the 21st Century*.
    2001   ISBN 90-411-1572-2

KLUWER LAW INTERNATIONAL — THE HAGUE/LONDON/BOSTON